DEDICATED

To my God, who is my life
To the people of Iceland, whom I have come to love
To my friends and family, who have, and continue to support me
To my church family, who continually pray for me

To you, Dear Reader, who is intrigued by what God is doing in the
country of Iceland

Table of Contents

FOREWORD:
WHY ME? WHY ICELAND?

Y ou may be wondering why I wrote this book. I wrote this book hopefully for the same reason you are reading it—because you are captivated by the good news of Jesus Christ and want to see all people come to faith in Him. As a member of the family of God, I hope that you yearn for people from other countries, made in the image of God, to be adopted into God's family. And one day, that family will finally be joined together from every tribe, tongue, nation, and people, standing before God's throne worshiping Him. (Rev 7:9-17)

Who am I? I am Aimee, a red-headed twenty-something who caught a vision of what God is doing in Iceland. I want to introduce you to the country and the people I have come to love and pray that you would also gain a heart to pray for this northern island of approximately 365,000 people.

In the coming pages, I will lay out a brief history that provides the context for the cultural landscape toward faith in Iceland, explore elements of the current Icelandic culture, and draw connections between Icelandic culture and barriers to the gospel. In the final two chapters, I will take a glimpse at the future to see what Christianity in Iceland might look like in the decades ahead, and finally, I will provide practical ways for you to get involved with the ministry in Iceland.

Before we dive into the history of this Nordic country, I would be remiss if I did not thank the many individuals who helped make this book possible. To Clint Clifton and Logan Douglas, thank you for your guidance, edits, and vision for this project, and for your continued faithful ministry in and for Icelandic people. To Gunnar Gunnarson, thank you for your willingness to share so much of your testimony, heart for ministry, and culture with me. I am incredibly grateful and pray your ministry continues to grow. To the many Icelanders who gave their time to talk to me—your willingness to share your stories provides hope for the gospel in Iceland, and I am incredibly grateful. To Paul Leidy and Robert LaHoud, thank you for your meticulous and faithful copy-editing. Without you both, I could never have brought this book to the finish line. And to my church family, Trinity Church of Loudoun, thank you for your faithful prayers and encouragement.

And to you, Dear Reader, I want to thank you for taking the time to learn about what God is doing in Iceland. As you read, would you consider praying for God to work salvation in Iceland? (Rom 1:16) Consider and ask the Lord how you can best serve your brothers and sisters in Iceland—you never know what God will do with imperfect but willing servants!

MY PRAYER FOR THIS BOOK

I f you spend enough time with me you'll find that I like quirky things—international music (German hip-hop is awesome, by the way), hole-in-the-wall restaurants, French movies—basically anything to prompt a story. Among the many stories I love are the Old Testament Prophets, which are some of my favorite books in the Bible.

I relate on a deeply personal level to the stories of two Old Testament prophets in particular—the story of Isaiah when he comes before God's throne and Jeremiah when God calls him to be a prophet. Isaiah catches a glimpse of the throne of God and His holiness and immediately cries "Woe is me! For I am lost; for I am a man of unclean lips, and I dwell in the midst of a people of unclean lips; for my eyes have seen the King, the Lord of hosts!" (Is. 6:5)

As a developing writer, I am extraordinarily conscious of how communication can go sideways and how my lips can be used for ill. In so many ways, I have unclean lips and my heart utters perverse and untrue things. I stand before God's holiness so broken, I feel unqualified to speak.

But I am reminded of God's grace, which covers my fears and proves to me time and again of His promises fulfilled. For Isaiah's uncleanness, an angel takes a burning coal from the altar before the throne of God and presses it to His lips, saying, "Behold, this has touched your lips; your guilt is taken away, and your sin atoned for." (Is 6:7 ESV) In the very same way, the Lord has reminded me constantly that He has taken away my guilt and atoned for my sin. By His grace I live, and by His grace I write this book.

In the story of Jeremiah, he is called to be a prophet at a young age. The Lord speaks to Jeremiah and assures him that since before he was born, God had set him apart to be a prophet. But Jeremiah is afraid and he tells God, "I do not know how to speak, for I am only a youth." God in his wisdom reminds Jeremiah:

Do not say, 'I am only a youth'; for to all to whom I send you, you shall go, and whatever I command you, you shall speak. Do not be afraid of them, for I am with you to deliver you. (Jer. 1:7-8)

I so relate to Jeremiah! I am only a youth—and can a twenty-something claim the wisdom of older generations? But here, God comforts me with His words. He says: Be not afraid. I have called you since before your life began. I have established this work for you to do. I will give you the words to speak. And when you become afraid, I am with you and will deliver you. If you know anything about God you know he keeps His Word, and so I trust that this promise is true. I am no prophet of Israel, I am no Jeremiah, but I am his adopted daughter and quietly trust him to guide me as faithfully as he guided Jeremiah.

And so, my prayer for this book mirrors the stories of Isaiah and Jeremiah. First, I pray that God would use my heart for the people of Iceland to communicate his grace. In the same way that Jeremiah was unqualified but God called him anyway, I pray that He would work through my weakness. Second, I pray that you would be encouraged by this book and inspired to pray for and support your brothers and sisters in Iceland.

Lord, I offer these words up to you and ask you to humbly take these words and transform them by your grace. May my words be for upbuilding in the body of Christ, not for tearing down, and may they be full of truth and grace. Where anyone could take offense, I pray that they might hear the love of Christ through these pages and catch a vision of your heart for Iceland.

I pray, most importantly, that you would be made much of in these pages, and that I would be made little. It's for your glory I live, and move, and have my being. It's for your glory that I write this book.

Amen.

1

THE LAND OF FIRE & ICE

When I stepped off the plane onto Icelandic soil for the first time in March of 2018, two realities instantly struck me: the wind was cold and the ground was warm beneath my feet. Part of the northernmost part of the European continent, Iceland is known as the "land of fire and ice" for a reason. With more than 130 volcanic mountains, Iceland is known for striking landscapes and extremes. The black volcanic earth peaks out among mossy grass that barely grows in the tough ground. Icy glaciers dot the rest of the northern island, where temperatures hover at the freezing point all winter. The contrasts continue—as a country within the Arctic Circle, Iceland receives nearly 24 hours straight of sunlight in the peak of summer, and approximately 6 hours of sunlight in the dead of winter. Iceland is otherworldly; waterfalls pour out of the heart of the volcanic island—along with scathing hot springs, precarious weather conditions, and sinkholes. Iceland holds this duality of both light and dark, beauty and danger, fire *and* ice.

Iceland captivated my heart that day. And even more than the beauty of the country, the people of Iceland stole my heart. I had been interested in Icelandic culture since a teenager, when I first discovered Icelandic music. The lyrics of *Sigur Rós's Hoppípolla* drew me in, with the playful theme of "jumping in puddles." I loved the creativity, the "northern-ness," and I wanted to learn more. My curiosity drew me to downtown Reykjavík, Iceland's capital city and largest town, to the famous Hallgrímskirkja (as hard to pronounce as it looks)—a church building that looks like a cross between a glacier and Elsa's ice palace in the movie *Frozen*. After getting my fill of pictures and seeing the inside of the building, I was struck by this question, "Are there gospel-believing Christians in Iceland?"

When I travel, I will sometimes sense a call to pray for the place I'm visiting—I've felt that call in large metropolitan areas like downtown L.A., Washington, D.C., and New York City, and in smaller cities like Lubbock, TX, and Mobile, AL. But all at once, the call to pray was overwhelming. It was so palpable and strong that I began to wonder *if* there were faithful Christians in Iceland. And I meant to find out.

As soon as I got home, I researched to find out what I could about this island suspended in the North Atlantic and what I found astonished me. While 65 percent of Icelanders are members of the State Lutheran Church, a fraction of them attend church with any regularity (somewhere between 0.2 and 2 percent of members attend services[1]).

But even church membership statistics are deceptive, since the State Lutheran Church preaches a message of moralism, while denying the authority of Scripture and of the deity of Jesus Christ. The University of Iceland houses the country's only seminary and teaches a theology curriculum that presents the Bible as a book riddled with errors that cannot be trusted. Since the church and state are intertwined in a complicated political arrangement, a degree in Theology in Iceland translates to a stable, government job.

As one of the most progressive countries in Europe, Iceland is currently undergoing the final stages of a cultural shift that has been ongoing since the turn of the 20th century—a shift away from traditional Icelandic Lutheranism and toward a kind of apathetic non-religion that is neither atheism nor paganism. It is simply irreligious, a shrug that says, "religion doesn't affect my life in any way, but if it works for you then that's cool."

In Iceland, the most recent generation to exhibit pious, committed faith was the generation born in the early 1900s, and have all passed on. I spoke with Helgi Hannesson, now in his 60s, about his testimony and what it was like for him to come to faith in Christ in Iceland. Though he was raised for the most part in the United States in the 50s and 60s, Helgi returned to Iceland for his college years. In the early 1970s, at 19 years old, he attended an evangelistic meeting at a Free Lutheran Church in downtown Reykjavík. There, he heard the message that he was a sinner and Christ had come to save him. He believed, and began fellowshipping with other believers at the University of Iceland.

Helgi eventually returned to the United States, where he met his wife, Guðrún, a fellow Icelander who had received Christ while visiting in California at the time. They were married in Iceland three years later, and the couple then lived in a number of countries so that Helgi could complete his graduate school education before returning to Iceland in the late 1990s.

When Helgi and Guðrún returned to Iceland, they looked around for a healthy church to join before settling on a small Brethren assembly with mostly Faroese and Icelandic couples. Eventually, they ended up joining Emmanuel Baptist Church, an English-speaking church that had been planted by American Baptist missionaries. The church congregation remained small through the late 2000s.

Several years later, after the last of the American missionaries who had pastored the church left Iceland, the small congregation of Emmanuel Baptist Church voted to merge with Loftstofan Baptistkirkja at the end of 2014. This infant church plant was pastored by Gunnar Gunnarsson, who founded it in 2013 with a handful of other couples. Helgi and Guðrun, who have at least two decades of seniority over the rest of the congregation, have been faithful members ever since.

Helgi and Guðrún's story illustrates an all too common reality among Christians in Iceland—the lack of available, gospel-preaching churches, and the lack of a mature generation of believers who have been walking with Christ for decades and can mentor and disciple others. Even writing those words breaks my heart! I pray often for the believers in Iceland who yearn for a Christ-centric, gospel-preaching church near to them but do not have access to one.

2

A BRIEF HISTORY

"Icelanders tend to resist being seen as descendants of the Vikings ... or as guardians of a deep-frozen 1,000-year-old Nordic culture. Nevertheless, we have a national self-image based on our historical heritage—the image of being a literary nation."

-Gunnar Karlsson,
A History of Iceland, page 361

I celanders have been preserving their history for five times as long as the United States was a nation. From the beginning of the Middle Ages (874 AD) to today, Icelanders have protected their heritage as a Nordic people. They recorded Norse mythology (when no one else did!), and even speak a modern version of the Old Norse language. Their history is well-documented for such a small country—we know more about random Icelandic farmers than we do Kings of England from the same time period—and their history often *rhymes* (as one of my professors in college used to say).[1]

Icelandic history is like a series of family trees that stubbornly grew in the harsh volcanic soil and, against all odds, survived other-worldly weather conditions. In other words, Icelanders have forged a history and society for more than a thousand years when most other people would have packed up and high-tailed it to some place—any place—more suited for human habitation.

In the following chapter, I will provide a 30,000 foot view of Icelandic history through an overview of the main events that have shaped modern Icelandic culture. The primary focus will be on the historical events in the State Church in Iceland that paved the way for the current climate toward Christianity. And, like the rest of their history, Iceland's relationship with Christianity is complicated.

Early Years: Iceland becomes a "Christian Nation" (874–1199)

Iceland was settled by Norwegian chief Ingólfr Arnarson and his fiefdom, a crew of approximately 400 farmers and settlers.[2] Rather than surrender to the ambitious King of Norway, Harald I Halfdansson (also known as Harald Fairhair), Ingólfr and his vikings fled across the North Atlantic Ocean to Iceland where they permanently settled. While they were the first official settlers on the island, historians recognize that more than 150 years earlier, Gaelic and Irish monks had begun to visit Iceland for reclusion and solace.

Twenty-five years before the first official settlement, another Norwegian viking named Naddodr set foot in Iceland and left his indelible mark on the virgin nation. He named the town of Reykjavík, which is now the country's capital city, after the "Smoky Bay" it surrounds. Today, Reykjavík is home to more than 120,000 Icelanders. Naddodr's success with naming the island ends there, however, because his alternative name for the country—Snæland or "Snow land"—did not stick.

By 930 AD, the population reached approximately 30,000 as more and more settlers emigrated to the country. The settlers formed their first parliament that year as well, organizing a constitutional commonwealth where elected members of the people served as members of the Alþingi ("Althingi" – Iceland's Law Gathering, akin to a parliament). Within those early years, Iceland established order with a law speaker, who memorized the entirety of Icelandic law and served as the final vote in divisive cases.

Just 70 years later, Iceland faced one such divisive case— that of whether or not to accept Christianity as the national religion. In the year 995, King Ólafur Tryggvason of Norway converted to Christianity and required all Nordic countries to convert as well. Over the next five years, he sent Norwegian Catholic priests to Iceland on three separate expeditions to convert the Icelandic chieftains.

While some chieftains did convert and were baptized into the Catholic church, others mocked the priests and paid a heavy price as a result. Bloodshed broke out between the priests and the chieftains forcing the Norwegian king to intervene. During a peaceful visit when converted Icelandic chieftains came to Norway, the king captured them and threatened execution if they did not convert their fellow chieftains.[3] In a desperate final plea, those chieftains negotiated with the king to let them return to Iceland to convince their fellow chieftains. The king agreed, but kept four of their sons captive in Norway.[4]

The issue of whether or not to accept Christianity as the national religion came to a head at the Alþingi the following summer, and two factions were divided on either side. With increasing pressure from Norway, the leaders of both factions left the final decision up to the lawspeaker. Ultimately, the Alþingi voted to compromise. They agreed that all of Iceland would convert to Christianity in order to appease the king of Norway, but would permit the following three activities in private:

1. They could still expose unwanted newborn children to the bitter cold, causing them to freeze to death, according to their old pagan religious practice.
2. They could eat horse meat, which was used in pagan sacrifice.
3. They could continue their practice of pagan sacrifices.[5]

Perhaps more than any other, this decision set the tone for Christianity in Iceland. Icelanders agreed to become Christians as *long as they could remain pagan* and forever established in the Icelandic consciousness that "I can accept

Christianity, but I have some conditions first." That same mindset appears throughout Icelandic history and continues in Iceland to the present day.

More importantly, this early decision to adopt Christianity came from the State, not from the Church. From its early beginnings, Iceland has had a state-run religion and in many ways, Iceland accepted Christianity as a political move with little spiritual transformation to accompany the decision.

While Christianity became increasingly important to the people of Iceland from the year 1000 onward, Christianity did not supplant the old love for the sagas and Norse mythology. In fact, some Icelanders continued to practice pagan sacrifice and worshiped the Norse gods in private, while publicly calling themselves Christians. Norse myths are woven into the tapestry of Icelandic history and culture—to the point that it can be difficult to distinguish between Icelandic history and myth through the Middle Ages. In some of the early sagas especially, Icelandic men and women complete quests and larger-than-life feats that only demigods could accomplish.[*1]

Christianity influenced the culture eventually, however, through the means of education. Iceland's first Christian bishop, Ísleifur Gissurarson, developed an Icelandic alphabet, founded a school, and trained his students in grammar and Latin. Because of this formative education provided by Ísleifur Gissurarson, Ari Þorgilsson "The Learned," learned to read and write and eventually recorded Icelandic history in *Íslendingabók* or *Landnámabók* (The book of Icelandic history, and the book of the Icelandic settlers, respectively). Without him, the Icelandic language and culture would not have been preserved.

Meanwhile, the daily life of Icelanders centered on survival. Icelanders fought the harsh winters and rugged terrain as if their lives depended on it, because they did. Food ran out in the first few winters and many died of starvation; farming was difficult so most subsisted on fish. Herring and cod were,

---

[*1] If Norse mythology intrigues you, I have summarized some pertinent myths in Appendix A.

and still are, staples of the Icelandic diet.

Because so little timber naturally grows on the island, most of the original Icelandic huts were constructed of dirt, not wood or stone. Icelanders built huts in a long line of rooms with a barn at one end so that animals could weather the cold winters, and they left enough space for cooking and sleeping at the other end. In these early years, Icelanders lived with a large extended family or shared their huts with other families. Huts were arranged close to each other for family members farming the same land. While family units lived very close to each other, Icelanders rarely clustered together in villages or towns, often living out of eyesight from the nearest cluster of huts.

Their struggle to survive developed into a kind of rugged independence and commitment to preserve their cultural heritage that is ingrained in the fiber of Iceland. Icelanders hesitate to change, probably because they excel at keeping alive a cultural heritage that others have abandoned a century ago.

Middle Ages: Priests, Politics, and the Plague (1200–1499)

If there was one word to describe Icelandic history over the next 300 years, it would be rocky. Throughout this time period, political struggles over property established tension between church and state. Iceland capitulated and declared allegiance to Norway, but then Norway shifted hands and became Denmark. To finish out the period, plagues ravaged Iceland and only a fraction of the population remained.

In 1269, power struggles between church and state escalated when the archbishop of Norway sent Bishop Árni Þorláksson with orders to take control of the tithes of the church. In his book *History of Iceland*, historian and expert on Icelandic life and culture, Gunnar Karlsson, writes that skirmishes between nobles and priests continued over the next few years, until the dispute was addressed at the Alþingi.

In 1270, the Alþingi ruled that real church property (i.e.

land) belonged to the church.[6] This is significant because over the centuries, the church gained more land rights until it owned more Icelandic soil than the state. As a result, at the beginning of the 1900s the Icelandic government struck a deal with the Church: they would pay the salaries of the priests as long as the church allowed them to build on church land. The relationship is now so intertwined that church and state would be quite difficult to separate.

The struggle over church ownership points to a deeper question in the Icelandic consciousness—the question of *who owns the church?* In many cases, local chieftains managed or "owned" the affairs of the church even though churches technically owned the property. Even from this early period, the affairs of the church were governed by chieftains and landowners and not primarily by the priests who, on paper, were the legal stewards.

During this time, the Lord's Supper was only consumed by the priest at the weekly mass. It was only on Easter that the population partook in the bread and wine of mass, giving local priests enormous spiritual influence over their congregations. Michael Fell, author of *And Some Fell Into Good Soil*, argues that Christianity in Iceland "became increasingly a religion of fear—fear of misfortune in this world and of damnation in the life hereafter."[7]

Simultaneously, Iceland was shifting politically. In 1302, they crafted an advantageous political union with their mother country, Norway. They were willing to swear allegiance to the King of Norway on one condition: only Icelanders could rule the internal affairs of Iceland.[8] This agreement solidified the political independence of Icelanders in their country while also protecting them from other countries that could have exploited the natural resources of the country.

Then, 80 years after Iceland came under Norwegian rule, one single heir was born to the thrones of both Norway and Denmark (intermarriage was at best, messy!). In 1376 King Olav, crowned King of Denmark at the age of 5 or 6 years old succeeded his grandfather to the throne, and four years later inherited the Norwegian throne upon his father's death in

1380. This boy king was more of a puppet than a true ruler, since his mother Queen Margrethe effectively ruled as regent for both countries.[9]

Over the years, Denmark exercised most of the leadership responsibility over Iceland, so when Norway separated from Denmark in 1814, Denmark maintained rulership over Iceland. This relationship continued well into the 20th century, with World War II (1944) marking the beginning of Iceland's complete independence as a sovereign nation and constitutional commonwealth.

Just as the political scene began to settle for Icelanders, the plague broke out—not just once, but twice! An unknown plague first showed up in Iceland in 1404, probably brought in by an import ship. Within the first wave of the plague, 50 percent of Iceland's population went to their graves. While their deaths left many farms and towns abandoned, plucky Icelanders rebuilt and within almost a hundred years had repopulated much of the island. Then, another 30–50 percent perished with a second wave of plague in 1495.[10] While likely not the Black Plague, this plague in Iceland was just as deadly. Icelanders were so terrified of death that some farmers dedicated their land to the church in an effort to save their souls.[11]

The Reformation, Iceland edition (1500–1799)

When Martin Luther nailed his 95 theses to the door of the Catholic All Saints Church in Wittenberg, Germany, he declared his disagreements with the practices of the Catholic Church. He criticized multiple church practices, including a stubborn commitment to conduct church services in Latin, and not in the language of the common man. With no way of understanding God's Word, the average person in Europe had no way of understanding the good news of Christ come to save. Luther sparked a fire that fanned the flame of reformation across Europe.

And yet, the Reformation itself presented a complex political shift. The Catholic Church had exercised *both* religious *and* political power over the kings of Europe at the time. So while the Reformation brought great change to the practice of Christianity within the church, it also prompted political upheaval across Europe. By reforming their churches and adopting Lutheranism (or any other form of reformed Christianity), they could disentangle their countries from the Pope's control.

When the newly crowned King Christian III of Denmark ascended the throne in 1534, he almost instantly adopted Lutheranism, making it the official religion in 1536. Lest you think this decision was religiously motivated, scholars agree that it was more likely a political move to unite his country after a civil war that he instigated.[12] His turn to Lutheranism allowed him to cut ties with Rome—waving a hearty goodbye to exorbitant tithes and outside political control.

Thus, Iceland *technically* became Lutheran overnight. In practice, however, it took almost a year for the first Lutheran priest to conduct a Lutheran service on the island. In 1537, the first Lutheran church service was performed in German in Hafnarfjörður.[13] It took another 50 years for Icelanders to have a reliable translation of the Bible in their own language, which allowed priests to conduct church services in Icelandic, as opposed to German, Dutch, or Norwegian.

An Icelandic Bible was one of the most significant benefits of the Reformation in Iceland. Between 1537 and 1540, Oddur Gottskálksson translated the New Testament into Norse (which has morphed into modern-day Icelandic), and published the first printed copy in 1540.[14] To date, Oddur's New Testament is the oldest printed book in Icelandic that has been preserved. In 1584, a new and improved translation of the Bible became available when Bishop Guðbrandur Þorláksson of Hólar bought a printing press, hired a typographer, and updated the 1540 translation. The final product was an ornately illustrated copy of the Holy Scriptures so rare that only 500 copies were printed. Each one sold for the steep price of two or three cows.[15]

Bishop Guðbrandur Þorláksson tried to further influence the Icelandic church by encouraging religious poetry. He hired poets and sagamen to compose religious poems, or rímur, long epic poems composed in strict verse. Oddur Gottskálks-son also prepared a set of Icelandic sermons called a postil, so that priests would have material to assist their sermons.[16] Guðbrandur and Oddur's efforts were so successful that the church obtained enough material to hold services in Icelandic, which Lutheranism required of the native tongue. This cemented Icelandic, not Danish, as the language of Iceland.

Icelandic poets continued to compose religious poetry throughout the centuries after the Reformation and contributed not only religiously but artistically as well. One of Iceland's most famous poets, Hallgrímur Pétursson, composed a set of poems titled *Passíusálmar* or "Hymns of the Passion" which is critically acclaimed as his greatest work. One of the poems in the collection, titled "The Purple Dress and the Crown of Thorns" is translated below:

> *Translation*
> Jesus was now to Pilate's hall
> By Roman soldiers taken.
> He stood there bare before them all,
> With courage still unshaken.
> A scarlet robe they clothed him in,
> And mocked Him, high above the din -
> Thus was my Lord forsaken,
>
> No robe I had to hide my shame,
> My soul stood all denuded.
> My sinful state from Adam came,
> From heav'n I was excluded.
> Sin's scarlet robe I clothed me in,
> Shame and reproach I found therein,
> My heart and mind deluded.
> But my dishonour passed away
> And my humiliation;
> He clothed my soul with bright array,
> The garments of salvation.
> Beneath His robe I refuge find
> And, in His righteousness enshrined,

Eternal consolation.[17]

Original
Illvirkjar Jesúm eftir það
inn í þinghúsið leiddu,
afklæddu fyrst og fljótt þangað
fólkið allt koma beiddu.
Purpuraklæðis forna flík,
fást mátti varla háðung slík,
yfir hans benjar breiddu.

Helgunarklæðið hafði eg misst,
hlaut því nakinn að standa.
Adam olli því allra fyrst,
arf lét mér þann til handa.
Syndanna flík eg færðist í,
forsmán og minnkun hlaust af því
með hvörs kyns háska og vanda.

Burt tók Jesús þá blygðun hér,
beran því lét sig pína.
Réttlætisklæðnað keypti mér,
kann sá fagurt að skína.
Athvarf mitt jafnan er til sanns
undir purpurakápu hans.
Þar hyl eg misgjörð mína

Fervent believers, such as Hallgrímur Pétursson served to transform the religious landscape of the time.

In the first century after the Reformation, a number of significant changes took place in Iceland. Church leadership abolished a number of practices that had become commonplace:

1. The dedication of churches to saints and to the Virgin Mary.
2. The veneration of images and saints.
3. Reading from a Latin Bible in services.

Instead, church services now centered around preaching and teaching God's Word in Icelandic. As a result, the reformation produced almost universal literacy in Iceland by the end of the 1700s, a status it maintains to this day.[18]

A few post-reformation priests stand out for their fervent faith and contribution to the spiritual heritage of Icelanders. One such spiritual giant, Guðbrandur Þorláksson (1542–1627), published approximately 90 books for Christian worship and edification. His work served to establish doctrine in Iceland, and flowed out of his own personal dedication to the Lord. Michael Fell writes, "He more than any other individual was responsible for the solid establishment of the Lutheran Church order and Lutheran orthodoxy in Iceland."[19]

A second priest of note is Jón Vídalín (1666–1720), who is famous for his collection of sermons that spoke directly to the daily life of Icelanders. Topics varied from the tragedy of losing loved ones, to the dangers of a seaman's life, to the self-indulgence of the rich that disregard the poor.[20] A master of the Icelandic language, his sermons had a high literary value and were so beloved that most households owned a copy by the year 1800. An excerpt from one of Jón Vídalín's sermons reveals a fervent and inspiring faith:

> When your heart burns within you (Luke 24) as God speaks to you in his word and you to him in prayer, when you pour out your heart before him and he pours back into it the consolation of his Spirit—in a word, when you feel in your heart love for God and for your neighbor (for these two cannot be separated)—when you feel all this, you may be perfectly sure that the entire Godhead in three Persons has taken up his dwelling with you; and you cannot possibly doubt the fact that you are a child of God (Romans 8).[21]

While significant changes within the Icelandic church directly resulted from the Reformation, the transition to Lutheranism was far from smooth in a political sense. In 1539, a bailiff and Lutheran named Didrich von Minden of Bessastaðir stormed the Catholic monastery in the region, stole food and livestock, defaced the monastery, and declared himself the ruler.[22]

Just a decade later in Skálholt, an Icelandic town nearly 95 km away (60 miles), a Catholic bishop led a counter-offensive. Bishop Jón Arason gained power over the diocese and was declared "the proper overlord of Christianity" at the Alþingi in 1550. The King of Denmark viewed the bishop's actions as a form of treason and captured Bishop Jón and his two sons a few months later, then beheaded them without a trial. Bishop Jón was declared a traitor and the King confiscated his property the following spring.[23] So while the Reformation brought many positive changes for religious fervor in the country, events like these were motivated more by political power than by religious fervor.

However, on a day-to-day basis for the average Icelander, life continued much as it had before. Icelanders gathered in the same churches, often with the same bishops and farm managers as before. The only differences were that now they conducted services in Icelandic and called themselves Lutheran.

A Catastrophic Era (1600–1899)

Following the Reformation, the 17th, 18th, and 19th centuries were filled with one catastrophe after another—pirates (you read that right!), volcanic eruptions, starvation, and a mass exodus.

Throughout their history, Icelanders have never maintained a standing army—the sons and daughters of vikings had little need for one. And for much of their history, it worked out pretty well for them. However, when pirates from the coast of North Africa landed on Icelandic shores, that was not one of those times.

These pirates came from the coast of modern-day Morocco, which was then part of the Ottoman Empire or "Turkish Empire." Also known as "Barbary Pirates" in other history textbooks, these unsavory individuals began to roam beyond the Mediterranean Sea into the North Atlantic. As the pirate ships crept closer and closer to Iceland, Icelanders prepared as best they could. The governor of the soutwestern region near Grindavík installed canons and built up a fortress near the harbor to ward off the invaders, but when the pirates got close to the shore, he chose not to open fire! Soon after, two more pirate shifts landed in the Eastern Fjords, capturing 110 people and killing at least 9.

The pirates then sailed for the Westman Islands, a set of mountainous Icelandic islands off the southwestern coast of Iceland. There, they captured 242 more people, killed 30-40 people, and burned churches and warehouses to the ground.[24] Few Icelanders defended their homeland against this attack. Instead, they put their energy into writing about it! A few self-educated farmers recorded the events of the raid in gory detail.

Life in Iceland continued to be a struggle throughout the 18th century—with three major catastrophes spanning the decade. The 1700s kicked off with an outbreak of smallpox that wiped out one quarter of the population.[25] The volcano Katla followed with a bang a few decades later. That eruption brought on multiple years of cold winters and poor catches of fish, leading to starvation. And in 1783, a second volcanic eruption spread poisonous ash and lava over the southwestern region, making farming in the area impossible, and causing brutal winters for the next few years. Poverty and famine spread throughout Iceland as cold winters consumed the limited stores of hay kept in reserve.

The volcanic ash expanded across Europe and produced small crop yields there as well, spreading famine and poverty to other European countries. In fact, some scholars believe the ash contributed to a poor harvest in France in 1785, leading to financial inflation and discontent among French peasants—the same peasants who welcomed the French Revolution just four years later in 1789.[26]

Life became so unbearable for Icelanders that some chose to flee the country in the early 1800s and sail for the United States and Canada. One of the significant migrations from Iceland to Canada established a colony dubbed "New Iceland" directly north of North Dakota, near Manitoba, Canada. The towns of Gimli and Thingvalla transplanted Icelandic culture to their new country, and even produced their own newspapers in Icelandic.[27]

All told, 17,000 Icelanders immigrated to America from 1870–1914, which was approximately 15 percent of the entire population in Iceland at the time.[28] Following the great migration, the end of the 19th century finished with another bout of calamities—a round of cold winters and an outbreak of the measles—ending the 19th century with a population of 70,000 in Iceland.

The Modern Period: Independence, U.S. and U.K. Involvement, and the 21st Century (1900–Current)

Like most other countries during this time, Iceland experienced rapid modernization throughout the twentieth century. Unlike other countries, however, they advanced from mud huts to modern conveniences in just a few decades. Iceland experienced numerous social shifts throughout the century, and most important of all was the shift regarding church and religion.

Between the end of the nineteenth century and the beginning of the twentieth century, Iceland experienced a sharp philosophical turn toward Rationalism, and adopted the view that all of reality must be explained rationally. With the advent of the University of Iceland in 1911, this philosophy of rational secularism quickly took root within the church and posed an antithesis to faith. Professor at the Seminary, Jón Helgason, began introducing German liberal theology and biblical criticism.[29] By the end of the 1920s, all priests in Iceland were required to graduate from one of the University of Iceland's theology programs in order to work as a state priest, effectively cementing liberal theology into the doctrine and practice of the Lutheran State Church.

A Movement of God in Iceland

Sparks of religious fervor came through the Salvation Army and YMCA (Young Men's Christian Association), which functioned more as churches than as humanitarian organizations in Iceland. In 1899, Icelander Friðrik Friðriksson founded the YMCA for students at the University of Iceland. Within a few years the YMCA became loosely connected to the YMCA in Denmark and participation grew. Friðrik invested in those who came to the YMCA meetings, and over the course of his life mentored many of the men and women who now hold leadership positions in churches and parachurch groups.

Just two decades later, another spiritual awakening was prompted when a Norwegian man named Eric Åsbo came to Iceland to preach the gospel. He had been transformed by a pentecostal revival that swept from Los Angeles's Azusa Street to Chicago, where he heard and believed.

Commissioned by a Swedish congregation, Eric and his wife arrived in Reykjavík in 1920, but his work there was unsuccessful, since another Icelander had started a ministry with the name of "Pentecostal" as well—but the ministry ended poorly. Thus, Icelanders shied away from the name "Pentecostal" and viewed Eric's ministry with suspicion.[30]

Then, in 1921, Eric and his wife travelled to the Westman Islands, a set of islands off the southwestern coast of Iceland (the same one the Turkish Pirates raided in the 1600s). Reports from his first open-air meeting say that 60 people committed their lives to Christ at the impromptu service.[31]

Bethel Pentecostal Church was then founded there in 1925, and one of those couples was Aron Hinriksson's great grandparents. Aron is now one of the co-pastors of Hvítasunnukirkjan Filidelfia (Brotherly

---

[2*] Independent Churches are not affiliated with the National Lutheran Church in Iceland.

Love Pentecostal Church), one of the largest independent Bible-teaching churches in Reykjavík today. Helgi Guðnisson great-grandmother was also baptized in 1925 at Bethel Pentecostal Church, and Helgi is now a co-pastor of Hvítasunnukirkjan Filidelfia.

Aron and Helgi are fourth- and fifth-generation sons, respectively, of leaders from this spiritual transformation, and they continue to pass along the faith to the next generation—through shepherding their flock, and through mentoring future pastors. And while faith is not genetic, they each expressed gratitude for their heritage of faithful followers of Christ.

And while Christianity flourished in the Westman Islands, independent churches[*2] in Reykjavík struggled throughout the second half of the twentieth century. Multiple churches experienced rapid growth followed by rapid decline. Whether due to failures by members in leadership, a lack of momentum from the congregation, or teaching contrary to Scripture being taught from the pulpit, these shrinking churches left a mark on Iceland as a whole. In some cases, they gave Christianity a bad reputation.

In the midst of this spiritual landscape, there are glimmers of hope and evidence of spiritual growth. Every year, the pastors at Hvítasunnukirkjan Filidelfia partner with churches around the country for a retreat where 1,500–1,800 will attend. Though not all of those individuals regularly attend church throughout the year, the pastors view it as a good sign that they are willing to spend a weekend in church community.[32] Helgi and Aron have also seen some promise in a mentorship program for individuals who are interested in becoming ministers. About 5–6 individuals are currently in the program, have been assigned to a mentor, and are receiving Bible training and character development.

Helgi and Aron meet to pray with pastors and Christians and desire spiritual growth to form wherever possible. However, they have seen an unfortunate tension in the National Lutheran Church, where "in general people don't see the church as a religious community, but rather an institution that just is."[33]

Throughout the twentieth century, the government and political arena in Iceland steadily improved. From the 1940s onward, Iceland gained political and economic independence and positioned itself as a country to be taken seriously in the 21st century.

When Germany invaded Denmark in 1939, Iceland took the opportunity to declare a separation from the mother country. On June 17, 1944, Icelanders made the separation official at the ancient site of the Alþingi. There, Iceland established a Constitutional Republic in the presence of a quarter of its population—a total of 25,000 people.[34] This new constitution was much the same as the previous one, except that Iceland elected a president to replace the role previously held by the King of Denmark. The President of Iceland holds no real veto power in the country, since any law a president refuses to sign will become provisionally valid until a referendum can confirm its validity.

Iceland's first test of their independence came in the form of the "Cod Wars," which were fought without the fire of a single bullet or the loss of a single soldier. In 1958, Iceland extended fishing waters to 12 miles from its shore. Britain was displeased with the arrangement, but ultimately accepted the boundary. Over the next 20 years, Icelandic and British fishing vessels clashed (literally!) over the fishing grounds as Iceland continued to expand its fishing borders until it reached 200 miles off the coast. Iceland's persistence in gaining control over fishing grounds proved successful, and on December 1, 1976, Icelanders gained complete control over their country's fishing grounds.

During World War II, the U.S. built a naval base at Keflavík in order to protect Northern Atlantic air routes. That base was abandoned in 1947, but was reestablished by the United States just four years later in 1951. Throughout the next 50 years or so (the base officially closed in 2006), American military men and women were stationed at Keflavík. And, as of June 2019, a declassified budget report shows the US investing $57 million toward improving the base, although there has been no official announcement about permanently stationing troops there.

The impact on Icelandic culture was significant—radio and TV stations, music, and imported food items all came as a result of the Americans "coming to town." An Icelandic writer for *The Reykjavík Grapevine*, Valur Gunnarsson, reflects back on the ways American culture influenced a generation of Icelandic writers, film-makers, and songwriters. He writes of the character Björk, who "wears American rubber boots and listens to Julie Andrews."[35] Gunnarsson concludes that, eventually, Icelandic culture conquered the English speaking world by taking refuge in Iceland's nature. Perhaps he's right? Considering the number of Americans fascinated by Icelandic culture and traveling in droves to see the gorgeous country, I think he has provided his point!

While the 2008 economic crash sent shockwaves through the international community, it devastated Iceland's economy. In October 2008, three of Iceland's banks collapsed into bankruptcy, leaving the country's entire financial system in collapse. The Icelandic Krona (ISK), the official currency of Iceland, is still recovering, and articles from Icelandic magazines are just now declaring a collective sigh of relief that the economy has recovered to pre-crash levels. Tourism contributed to the economy stabilizing, as the number of people currently employed by the tourism industry has doubled in the last 10 years.

Observations

In looking at the entirety of Icelandic history, it is easy to see why these creative and self-reliant people fought to gain independence for their Northern island. Even though the winters are hard, making a living is difficult, and every hundred years or so a volcano erupts and shrouds the country in ash, it nevertheless remains one of the most beautiful countries in the world.

In their checkered past with Christianity, Icelanders have a few gems of fervent faith wedged in between a rockbed of cultural apathy. It is those gems that stand out to me when I reflect back on the history of Iceland, and I wonder—what if the future of Iceland is not like the past? What if, this time around, Icelanders accept faith in Christ on no conditions. With such grit and tenacity, I can just imagine how Icelanders would dedicate themselves completely to the grace of Christ.

And yet, how Icelanders respond to the gospel is fundamentally tied to their history. Modern Icelandic culture flows from their history, and provides clarity for how Icelanders are likely to respond to the gospel today.

3

CURRENT CULTURAL FACTORS

"I think Icelanders are still Nomads, waiting for the sky to tell them whether they will go fishing tomorrow. You never plan because you wait for what the clouds will tell you."

-Helgi Guðnason, co-pastor of Hvítasunnukirkjan Fíladelfía (Brotherly Love Pentecostal Church)

Icelanders live in a world of contrasts. Survivors of more than 1,000 years of frigid winters, Icelanders possess the internal fire of self-reliance, independence, and pride for their country—and yet, are simultaneously chill. Fire and ice coexist here as well. Icelanders have vikings for their ancestors and the fierceness to match, but they also epitomize what you might feel while lounging on a Caribbean beach, sipping a mango smoothie. Iceland is an island country after all.

The contrasts continue; Iceland is traditional yet progressive. While Iceland has preserved history and tradition for centuries—the Icelandic language is one prime example—it has also become one of the most proudly progressive countries in Europe.

That progressivism spills over into the realm of religion, so while Christianity is publicly supported by the state government, Icelanders would admit to attending church only a mere handful of times over their lives. Though they call themselves Christians, by and large, Icelanders practically see church as a place for good children's programming more than anything else.

With so many contrasts present in Iceland, it is difficult to pinpoint the main cultural factors present within the country. I feel self-conscious even attempting to write this chapter as an American and am deeply conscious of my own limited perspective. If someone from another culture came to the United States to write about the culture and state of the church in the U.S., I am sure I would cringe and read it with two heaping tablespoons of skepticism.

My hope is that this chapter presents a balanced, fair, and impartial view of the main aspects of Icelandic culture. I am certain that not *all* Icelanders exhibit every trait identified in this chapter, in the same way that I know for a fact that not *all* Americans are loud, opinionated consumers who love their McDonalds, Walt Disney, and Monday Night Football.

These four aspects of Icelandic culture are not meant to be exhaustive; they are simply meant to be an introduction so that you as the reader might be better equipped to pray and minister the gospel among these beautifully complex people.

1. Creativity

First and foremost, Icelanders are a creative people and are proud of their literary heritage. When Icelanders settled their island country, they immediately set to work recording their history through stories and poems, and chronicled Norse mythology. There is a reason why the only original source of Norse mythology was written by an Icelander—they prize storytelling.

Icelandic history and Norse mythology are woven together in a cultural fabric that forms the backdrop for the culture today. The Norse myths are not "historically true *per se*" in Icelanders' minds, but they form a shared heritage built into the foundation of their society. The *Prose Edda* records the tales of the Norse gods, who exhibit some of the same human qualities shared in the Greek pantheon. Abbie Farewell Brown, editor of *Norse Mythology: Tales of the Gods, Sagas, and Heroes* describes the Norse pantheon as "often selfish, petty and quick to anger, but they could also display great generosity and were prepared for immense sacrifice."[1] Thor, the god of thunder, is both courageous and prone to rage. Loki, god of cunning, is both crafty and a lover of music and art. Odin, the father of the gods, is wise but selfish and prone to overlook the faults of his children.

The Norse pantheon even affects English culture on a daily basis: the English days of the week are named for Norse gods. Sunday is Sul's Day, Monday is Mani's Day, Tuesday is Tyr's Day, Wednesday is Woden's Day (Odin's Day), Thursday is Thor's Day, and Friday is Freya's Day. Saturday, or Saturn's Day, is the only day that *doesn't* come from Norse mythology; instead it comes from Roman mythology.

When reading tales of Norse Mythology, some similarities emerge between Christian and Norse heritage. In some tales, it appears that by the time Snorri Sturlsson recorded the Norse myths, Christian ideas had become intertwined with the old tales. Because the myths were recorded more than 100 years after Christianity was adopted in Iceland, historians have suggested that the authors mingled Christian themes into the myths to redeem them or graft them into the new, Christianized view of the world. To read a summary of a creation, redemption, or end of the world myth, see Appendix A.

While the sagas record the valiant feats of vikings in early Icelandic history, Icelanders are more likely to write poetry or a travelogue than they are to fight. Icelanders as a whole value creativity over confrontation.

There are a number of examples of this throughout their history, and the most notable is from 1627 when Barbary Pirates raided Iceland. More than 300 Icelanders were captured or killed during the raid on the southwestern coast of Iceland, yet no cannon shots were fired, and Icelanders as a whole did not fight back. Only a few dozen Icelanders survived their capture to Morocco, but many of them recorded their saga when they returned.

Icelanders were so good at recording their everyday lives that we know more details about random Icelandic farmers in the 900–1200s AD than we do the kings of Britain during the same period. For Icelanders, anyone could be the hero of their own story. An Icelander was noble, and his story was worth telling well. The sagas highlight feats of bravery, courage, and everyday life as a means to highlight the skill of their author or poet. "Saga-men," as they were called, were the most revered men of Icelandic society. To be a great storyteller was to be a great Icelander.

In that sense, Icelanders prize their artists more than their businessmen, politicians, or academics. Their artists are the people they would say are the best representatives of Icelandic culture. Today, that translates to the worlds of film, music, and literature.

As authors, Icelanders are quite accomplished, and their identity as a literary nation is something they value. Every year, between 1,000 and 1,500 books are published in Iceland by Icelandic authors, with most published just in time for Jólabókaflóðið ("the book flood") at Christmastime. Icelanders historically give each other books as Christmas presents—whether they read them is another question entirely. Nonetheless, for the entire week between Christmas Day and New Year's Day, it is a tradition for people in Iceland to stay home and read books.

Though Icelanders always knew they were a creative literary people, it wasn't until 1955 that they saw recognition for their talent on the world stage. In that year, Halldór Kiljan Laxness won the Nobel prize for literature for his book *Salka Valka*, which had been adapted for film in 1954. During the Nobel Prize presentation speech, Swedish Academy member E. Wessén began with what every Icelander already knew to be true, saying "Iceland is the cradle of narrative art here in the North."[2]

Another way that Icelanders preserve their literary heritage is through the education of their youth. Throughout Iceland's history, the people have been recognized for their literacy and quality of education, regardless of the socioeconomic status of their parents. Education in Iceland has transcended the division of class and social hierarchy so that even the children of poor sheep farmers know how to read, write, and more importantly, tell stories.

Icelandic education was so historically renowned that even rural New Yorkers in the town of Middletown, New York were aware of it. In 1860, the Middletown newspaper the *Banner of Liberty* translated and read a report on Iceland at one of their meetings. The article suggested that "the long winter nights made the people poetical," and the writer was shocked to discover that "the fathers teach their children so effectually, that a young Iceland boy or girl eight years old cannot be found who does not know how to read and write."[3] Iceland's status as a literate nation continues to the present—the country boasts a literacy rate of 99 percent among all Icelanders 15 years or older.[4]

In music and film, Icelanders are emerging as seminal creators. Take for example film composer Ólafur Arnalds, who composed the hauntingly beautiful soundtrack for the BBC series Broadchurch. Or, the various Icelandic creatives involved in acting and production for *The Girl with the Dragon Tattoo* in both Sweden and the U.S. Still more successful are a number of Icelandic bands, including *Of Monsters and Men*, *Sigur Rós*, and *KALEO*.

To read more about Icelanders in film and music, see Appendix B. For a list of critically acclaimed Icelandic literature, music, films, and actors, see the Resources guide at the end of this book.

With such a literary and creative people, who knows what the next quarter of a century holds in store for Icelandic creatives? Perhaps they will be recognized with a level of prestige in the realms of art, fashion, design, and more. It is just a matter of time for this creative people to find their voice on the world stage.

2. Fierce Independence

While Icelanders are well known for their creativity, there is a reason why one of Nobel Laureate Halldor Laxness's novels was titled *Independent People*. Icelanders are seminally creative, yes, but they are even more thoroughly independent.

As the children of the frozen winters of the North, Icelanders have had no one to rely on but themselves to preserve a culture through more than a century of harsh living conditions. They have cultivated land that most others would have abandoned immediately—their volcanic soil rejects most fruits and vegetables and barely produces a wheat crop. Not much grows on the island besides a thick undergrowth of moss, and even trees are sparse. Between volcanic eruptions and the volcanic soil, the country's native aspen trees hardly cover one quarter of the island's entire topography. With such a harsh environment, it's clear to see why Icelanders would develop such ingrained independence and self-reliance.

Their self-reliance extends to traditional Icelandic fare, which in at least one case would otherwise be poisonous to eat. A quick google search of "Traditional Icelandic Food" yields some terrifying results:

Hákarl (Fermented Shark)
Súrir hrútspungar (Sour Ram's Testicles)
Harðfiskur (Dried fish)
Svið (Sheep's head)
Slátur (Blood Pudding)

For Icelanders, no food was wasted because there was so little to go around. Truly, I would rather live in any other place and time than Iceland in the middle of winter in 1250 AD.

Life was so hard on the northern volcanic island that the entire population faced starvation, death, and disease multiple times. From the plague of the 1400s, to volcanic eruptions, to the frigid winters of the eighteenth and nineteenth centuries, to food shortages, and subsequent mass emigration—there were many points in Icelandic history where a less fiercely independent people would have packed up their belongings and abandoned Iceland for good.

Icelanders also fought fiercely for their political independence. Originally established as a commonwealth in 974 AD, the Icelandic people did everything within their power to retain their autonomy even after declaring fealty to the King of

Norway in 1302. At multiple points in Iceland's history, the Alþingi passed legislation and amendments to their constitution that separated Iceland from the direct jurisdiction of the kings of Norway and Denmark. Thus, Iceland's internal affairs have always been managed by Icelanders. Denmark did little to curb or shape that identity. Though at various points they could have sent an army to protect Iceland (i.e. when the Barbary Pirates ravaged the coast), Denmark chose to stand back and observe the chaos. This lack of outside protection bred a kind of rugged independence that preserved the Icelandic way of life to the present day.

Proud of their nation's heritage, Icelanders fiercely cling to their cultural identity. A fairly homogeneous group of Viking descendents, the nation maintains a population of only 365,000 people. With such small numbers—Icelanders joke that over all of Icelandic history there have only been one million Icelanders ever to live—the Icelandic people cherish a singular identity as a people, and as a nation. This Icelandic ethnic pride provides all that an Icelander needs in the realm of identity and says: "We are Icelanders; we need no other name." For a select few, this includes their Viking heritage, but that remains a minority, and is primarily found among Icelandic men.

A still smaller number of Icelanders look back to their pagan religious roots and are followers of a recent resurgence of the Norse religion, called Ásatrú (pronounced "Ow-saw-true"). For most of these followers, their exploration of Norse mythology represents a desire to connect with their Icelandic roots more than it does a conversion to a pagan religion. In this way, Icelanders exert their independence as a culture by maintaining the old traditions and the old religion.

Icelanders are self-reliant in their independence, partly because they have no other choice. The cost of living is high in Iceland—almost everything has to be imported, except for fish—so most Icelanders work hard to make ends meet. As one Icelander aptly put it in an interview, "They're not 'cry in my beer kind of people', they are 'solve my problems myself' kind of people."[5]

3. Progressive (and proud of it!)

As independent people, Icelanders are not fond of boundaries or limits on their sense of identity, and as such, they are particularly interested in being progressive, egalitarian, and non-judgmental.

Icelandic last names are one recent example of Iceland's progressivism. Traditionally, Icelandic last names are patronymics (or matronymics in some cases), meaning they take the father's (or mother's) first name and add "dóttir" or "son" to it. In June 2019, Iceland's Alþingi passed the "Gender Autonomy Act" that allows men and women to have names that have traditionally been reserved for the opposite gender. To accommodate people who identify as non-gender binary, the Act also permits individuals to identify their gender as "X" on official documentation and to change their last name to the ending "-bur" instead of "-son" or "-dóttir."[6] This change is more symbolic than anything, as Icelanders rarely refer to anyone by last name. For simplicity's sake, all Icelanders are referred to by their first name, even the Prime Minister. This breeds a kind of individual, egalitarian identity where every Icelander is treated with equal value.

In Icelandic sagas, you see the roots of egalitarianism in the first fibers of Icelandic culture. Many sagas highlight the bravery of men *and* women. These women stand tall in history, even when their husbands had little to say for themselves. This deeply rooted egalitarianism, though often noble, has now shifted to embrace all sexual identities and preferences in the last fifty years.

Iceland's gay pride is celebrated openly. In 2009, Iceland became the first country in the world to elect an openly homosexual head of government. Jóhanna Sigurðardóttir, a self-proclaimed lesbian, was elected prime minister in 2009 after serving nearly 30 years in the Icelandic Parliament. Additionally, in 1980 Iceland became the first country in the world to democratically elect a female president, Vigdís Finnbogadóttir.

Among the average Icelander, this egalitarianism means

a kind of laxity regarding institutions such as the family. Few Icelanders get married, and instead live together in a form of domestic partnership to raise children. This breakdown of family relationships leads Europe with the highest percentage of children born out of wedlock, a stunning 67 percent.[7]

Parenting methods are relaxed in general and corporal punishment (spanking, for example) has been outlawed since 2003.[8] That said, this laid-back approach to parenting comes with significant benefits. Children are given freedom to explore, and when I visited Iceland I saw the beautiful results of this practice. Children played, walked around the room, and danced to music without being shushed or corralled.

And yet, there are some downsides to this lack of parental oversight. As Icelandic children grow up with few constraints to curb their curiosity, many begin experimenting with alcohol, drugs, and sex at a young age. There appears to be a casual expectation that young people will experiment with drugs, sex, and alcohol without attaching any shame attached to those activities. An Icelander might shrug and say, "What's the big deal? Experimenting with sex, drugs, and alcohol is just part of growing up."

Due to all of these factors, a biblical view of morality and sexuality is a *huge* stumbling block for many Icelanders exploring orthodox Christianity. And given their frankness, Icelanders will not wait around to talk about it. Icelandic pastor Gunnar Gunnarson tells stories of Icelanders who have asked him questions about homosexuality, sexuality, abortion, and other controversial topics the first time they met. "Generally if you hold to biblical views with regards to sexuality, abortion, or anything controversial, you're quickly branded a bigot and a hater," Gunnar said.[9]

4. Happy ... (and the most depressed?)

Icelanders are proud to live on their island and think it to be the "best place the sun shines on."[10] By their own admission, they are some of the happiest people on the planet. The United Nations' "World Happiness Report" lists Iceland as the fourth happiest nation in the world as of March 2019.[11] All the Nordic countries vie for the top spot, with each of the past five years listing Denmark, Norway, Iceland, and Finland among the top. However, Iceland also has a dark side. Not only do they spend their winters shrouded in darkness (they get a mere 6 hours of daylight in the dead of winter), but they also lead the world with the use of antidepressants. This duality of happiness and depression is prevalent throughout Icelandic culture.

As for what sparks their happiness, Icelanders love the natural beauty of their island, and point to it as one of the major contributors. In taking a quick tour of the country and seeing firsthand the stunning geysers, glaciers, fjords, beaches, and mountains—the landscape speaks for itself. Iceland is a beautiful island full of natural resources and a vibrant ecosystem. Easy access to volcanoes, geysers, and hot springs that dot the island have attracted more than just locals. Tourism has exploded in recent years, now that the world is aware of Iceland's untouched, rugged beauty. From Thingvellir National Park, to countless waterfalls, to the Westfjords, the Icelandic countryside is drop dead *gorgeous*.

The beauty of Iceland and the lifestyle of Icelanders produces a kind of unhurried *chill*. Most Icelanders live so close to where they need to go that they do not venture far. A twenty-minute drive is about as far as any Icelander will travel on a regular basis, and so mealtimes are casual and relaxed. When I was in Iceland, I always expected dinner to take a minimum of two hours, and everyone around me expected that as well. The majority of Icelanders are not slaves to clocks or schedules.

Both the beauty of the island and the unhurried lifestyle contribute to Icelanders' happiness. They are simply less stressed than the average overworked American. In addition, they are simply proud of their island and want to share their beautiful country with others. When tourists come to visit, they are friendly. Often an Icelander will ask "why did you choose to come to Iceland, of all places in the world?" They love their corner of the world and want everyone else to know how beautiful it is.

But in the same way that this beautiful country is under-girded by dark volcanic soil, the Icelandic people live with a happiness that thinly veils a deep-seated darkness. The winters are long and cold, and Icelanders often isolate themselves from their neighbors, choosing to keep their struggles private. Others live isolated lives in tiny villages cut off from the rest of the country. Taken together, the long winters and independent culture breed a kind of deep-seated loneliness and depression that covers the country like a blanket for months of the year. Seasonal depression sets in with the winter and all are affected by it.

Icelanders maintain a perplexing duality—they are *both* happy and depressed. Part of it may come from Icelanders honesty and frankness. They are not self-deceptive people and are willing to admit that human experience includes both happiness and sadness. That said, they are still unlikely to talk about the darker side of their experience. As private, reserved people, they are more likely to quietly muscle through their depression than open up about it.

Their depression also comes from a sense of loneliness and spiritual darkness present within the culture of Iceland. While Icelanders are content to live on their island, they do not always invest in the people, friendships, or communities surrounding them. In Iceland, it is rude to wave at each other or meet each other's gaze on the sidewalk because that would be an intrusion, an invasion of privacy. In fact, Icelanders can be put off by people who show more affection than they are accustomed to express. They are private, unassuming, shy people. It catches Icelanders a bit off guard when gregarious Americans come, look them in the eye, and envelop them in a hug.

International statistics further reveal the dark side of Icelandic society. As indicated earlier, the Organization for Economic Development (OECD) reports that Iceland leads the world in antidepressant use, with approximately 14 percent of the country prescribed a daily antidepressant. Iceland has remained at the top of that list for years, so this is not a new phenomenon. A number of writers have offered suggestions as to why antidepressant usage might be so high. Forbes writer Niall McCarthy suggests that the increase in antidepressant use could be traced to the financial collapse of 2008, when all three of Iceland's banks failed.[12] An article by *Business Insider* posits that Iceland could over-prescribe antidepressants, since there is little social stigma associated with taking one.[13] Either way, antidepressants are prevalent in Iceland and many struggle with depression, anxiety, and a variety of other mental health issues.

Susceptibility to depression is present throughout the culture, but is especially prevalent among teenagers. As of 2015, Iceland took second place worldwide for the most teenage suicides. Before diving into the report, it is worth mentioning that the small population in Iceland does alter the statistics, since Iceland's population is compared against countries like Russia, China, and the United States. That caveat aside, depression is a significant issue for the teens in Iceland, and for Iceland as a whole.

The OECD released a report on the issue of teenage suicide globally in 2017. According to their report, Iceland saw 18 teenage suicides per 100,000 teenagers in 2015, 23 teenage suicides per 100,000 teenagers in 2000, and 28 suicides per 100,000 teenagers in 1990.[14] The report is revealing: not only does Iceland take second place for the highest number of teenage suicides, but teenage suicides in Iceland spike once every decade and have for the past thirty years. This issue is a systemic problem, not just a recent development.

This factor is honestly portrayed in the short film *Whale Valley* (2015). The film focuses on the issue of teen suicide from its opening scene where younger brother Ívar unexpectedly walks in on his older brother Arnar's suicide attempt. The boy does not go through with his intended plan after his younger brother walks in on him, but the film nevertheless continues with a somber tone. The isolated landscape, raw beauty of the remote fjords, and wildness of Icelandic animals all contrast sharply with the older brother's struggle with depression and suicide. The two boys experience life alone, isolated without the support of their parents.

In an interview with Vimeo about the inspiration for the film, Director Guðmundur Arnar Guðmundsson reveals that the story was very personal for him. A few of his friends committed suicide as teens, and he wrote the story to process his own grief. Guðmundur's description of what it was like to grow up in Iceland and encounter suicide as a teen reveals much about how the culture of Iceland responds to the issue:

> *I've had a few friends that have taken their own lives so that is the reason why I wanted the film to partly deal with that subject. Also, growing up in Iceland, back then, it was considered a weakness for boys to show their emotions and I think that very much affected me. I learned to keep things in and my escape route became the nature that I would seek to mirror my emotions.[15]*

A further proof of the underlying darkness present within Icelanders is their sense of humor. The Icelandic sense of humor is dark, morbid, and sarcastic. Take for example the comedic short film *Milk and Blood* (2014), which features a father and son dairy farmer duo. The film opens with an angry outburst from the father because his stupid and forgetful son did not connect the dairy machines to the holding tank for milk. The entire night's milk supply was wasted, spilled all over the floor.

In a sudden burst of anger, the son slams the stainless steel milk tank door on his father's head, and he keels over, dead. Stunned, the son drags his father's body to an empty cow stall to figure out what to do next. Just then, the doorbell rings—the milk delivery truck had just showed up. By the time the son returns, his father is gone! Terrified of what his father will do to him, the son takes off running through the fields outside the farm while his father chases after him.

The son turns abruptly to face his father and grabs him by the neck in an exaggerated, melodramatic face-off. The son wrestles his father to the ground and in one tear-filled moment, chooses not to strangle his father to death. He extends his hand to his father, lifting him up to his feet. The father then grabs his son by the shoulder, and the two of them stroll back to the farm as if nothing had happened. The son asks "Where were you running off to?" The credits roll.

Did I mention that *Milk and Blood* is a comedy?! This short film was popular—and featured at the Reykjavík, Chicago, Atlantic, Florida, and Interfilm Berlin Film Festivals. It even won the Topanga, CA film festival. According to Icelander and pastor Gunnar Gunnarsson, *Milk and Blood* is the norm for Icelandic media: "Icelandic movies are all very dark. Somebody always dies. They have a dry, morbid, sarcastic sense of humor."[16]

To watch the Icelandic films mentioned here, or to find more suggestions, see the Additional Resources section at the back of this book for some titles.

Conclusion

Icelanders have many traits that make them a unique, fascinating group of people. Their insatiable creativity, independence, self-reliance, and reserve make for an endearing mix. While they may be a bit standoffish and difficult to get to know at first, once they become friends, they are friends for life. If only Christ would transform this independent people by the power of His good news! Once set free from sin, Icelanders will be so fundamentally transformed by God's grace that they will cling to it with every fiber of their being.

The main difficulty in getting to that point of spiritual transformation is breaking past decades of cultural apathy. And while there are other barriers to the gospel, apathy rises to the top as the main hindrance. Join me in the next chapter as we explore how these cultural factors in Iceland produce distinct barriers to the spread of the gospel.

4

BARRIERS TO GOSPEL PROGRESS

"Iceland is not atheistic, it's apathy-istic."

-Sindri Guðjónsson,
President of Iceland's Atheist Association, Vantrú

The president of Iceland's Atheist Association described Icelanders perfectly by calling out their religious expression as one of apathy. It's not that Icelanders are anti-religion; most simply do not care about religion. Across Iceland, people adopt a kind of shrug toward religion that says, "eh, if it works for you, great. But religion just isn't my thing." Combine that with a progressive society that accepts every lifestyle and you find that most Icelanders have no need for God, at least not on the surface. And still others think they are already Christians because they are members of the National Lutheran Church, officially known as the Evangelical Lutheran Church of Iceland.

The barriers to the gospel in Iceland are not incredibly different from the barriers present within any country—sin rears its ugly head in Iceland as it does in every place. However, a few themes emerge more frequently in Iceland than they do in other countries. To illustrate some of the common barriers, let me introduce you to some typical Icelanders. The first thing you notice about **Kristín Björg Karlsdottír** is her infectious smile, shining a bit of sunshine on each moment as if it was one of her particular favorites. I met with Kristín in the kitchen and living room of her home, filled with the scattered remains of cheerios and favorite toys—the tell-tale signs of a life that three young children bring. Now in her late twenties, Kristín reflected on how she came to believe in God and trust Jesus as her Savior at the end of her high school years, when she had a *lot* of misconceptions about Christianity.

Though she was confirmed in the national church at fourteen years old, like most of her friends, she knew next to nothing about the Bible and was far from trusting God at the time. In fact, she thought that God was a cosmic pervert. Her logic went like this: "If God can see everything in the world, then he can also see everyone in the shower." Yet in the midst of her teenage doubts, she remembers the sense that God was real, even if she suppressed that sense until a few years later.

At fifteen, a friend invited her to a youth event at a Pentecostal church and after that event, Kristín kept coming back to church. She connected with other teenagers her age in the church and eventually began following the blog of a guy named Friðberg, who blogged about his experiences at a Bible College in the United States. Kristín remembers following that blog and thinking to herself *"this guy is so extreme."* At the time, Kristín did not know any other Icelanders who actually believed the Bible to be true or who were excited about church. Christianity intrigued her, in part, because it was not mainstream. Fast forward two years and as soon as Friðberg returned to Iceland, they started talking and eventually began dating and living together.

While they were living together, the Lord convicted Kristín through a sermon she saw online. In it, Paul Washer preached to a youth conference in the United States and challenged them with the message that "just because you attend church, you do not necessarily know God." Through that sermon, Kristín was convicted and repented of her sin. "All of a sudden, I was thinking differently. I was living in sin, so I just couldn't do it anymore. We broke up."

Meanwhile, God was working in Friðberg's life. One night he awoke and felt an overwhelming need to read the Bible, as if God was waking him up in order to read the Bible. He opened the New Testament and started reading Matthew. While reading, God opened his eyes to the gospel and he believed. The next day he came to Kristín, they started dating again (without living together this time) and were married seven months later. "God has done a miracle in our lives. We are not the same people," Kristín said.[1]

Now a committed follower of Christ, Kristín has shared the gospel with her family members who have responded in a variety of ways. Their posture toward religion in general, and Christianity specifically, is revealing.

In a conversation in the summer of 2018, Kristín's father brought up church in order to explain all of his problems with the church, and was shocked that Kristín actually believes the Bible. For him, faith is nominal, nothing more than tradition and morality: "He knows we go to church every Sunday, but he doesn't realize we really believe. He thinks we're like other Icelanders who go to church on Easter," Kristín said. Kristín has also shared the gospel with her mom, who took the message well, but did not respond in faith. Her mom agrees to disagree, and avoids 'stirring the pot,' choosing not to engage in the discussion.

One of her brothers became angry when Kristín told him about the gospel. He did not understand why he should believe in the Bible and give up his lifestyle. "If you believe in Christianity, it's boring and you can't do all the things you want to do." Similarly, her sister believes she's a Christian because she sometimes prays. But when Kristín told her that Christians should not have sex before marriage, she responded, "Why would God care about that? I think he doesn't care if I have sex before marriage."

In addition to her family members, the Icelanders surrounding Kristín think that Christians who take the Bible seriously are extreme. "You can have religion and you can go to church, but if you take the Book seriously, then you're taking it too far," she told me, relating comments that she had received. Furthermore, Kristín has found that fellow Icelanders are largely unaware of what the Bible teaches and have their own ideas about what Christianity is. "They have no idea that they have sinned, personally. They know Christ died for their sins, but they don't know what sins they have committed or what sin means," she said.

Kristín's story illustrates many barriers to the gospel spreading in Iceland, but the primary barrier she faces is one of apathy. In Iceland, the majority do not care enough to think about religion, much less change their lifestyles because of religious belief.

Barrier 1: Apathy

For the majority of Icelanders, Christianity is relegated to the realm of tradition. In fact, Icelanders are automatically assigned membership to the same church where their parents are members, as long as both parents are members of the same church. This produces a mindset that "to be Icelandic is to be a Christian." A large percentage of all Icelanders are baptized in a national church, confirmed at age fourteen in a national church, married in a national church, and buried by the national church. In the days between those key life events, most Icelanders will never darken the door of a church and even fewer will crack open a dusty Bible to read it for themselves.

While membership in the Evangelical Lutheran Church of Iceland currently rests at 65 percent of the country's population (or 227,000 people), a fraction of the population actually attend church. Based on numbers publicly available via *Statistics Iceland* in 2019, somewhere between 0.2–2 percent actually attend church (anywhere from 474–2,613 individuals).[2] Furthermore, low church attendance is not a new phenomenon. Since the early 20th century, church participation averaged under 10 percent of the population, even though 99.5 percent of Icelanders were members of the national church of Iceland at that time.[3,4] Today, that means that even in the country's largest churches, the pews will be dotted with about 20 people!

Icelanders live their lives as functional atheists, in that

God does not affect their everyday lives. With that context as the foundation, is it any surprise that Icelanders look at Christians and shrug? Their philosophy is consistent with the way they live their lives: *You do what you want, believe what you want, live your own truth, and I do the same.* Even this philosophy may be overstated, since Icelanders view religion with a *don't rock the boat mindset.* As casual religious pluralists, most Icelanders do not take the time to figure out what they believe.

The most common response to the gospel is not antagonism; it's apathy. Pastor Gunnar Gunnarsson said that the apathy present in Iceland is palpable. While Icelanders are unlikely to be hostile, they are "people who just don't care what you have to say."[5] The most likely response is a shrug and, *that's great, that works for you.*

Apathy is doubly present in Iceland, not only in the way Icelanders approach religion, but in their lives overall. Icelanders, in general, have a more relaxed temperament than other Western cultures. Where an American might have a 5-year plan and a schedule with lunch and dinner meetings booked for the next month, the average Icelander will be hesitant to set up a coffee date with a friend and instead will shrug and say "this will work out." Icelanders generally do not fill their schedules with appointments or stress about being on time. While that means they are good at living in the moment and appreciating the beauty of their island, it also predisposes them not to consider the future. The average Icelander approaches religion with a lifestyle of apathy or even an "I'll figure out what I believe someday," so the idea of changing their lifestyle to align with something they believe is a foreign concept for most.

Barrier 2: Nominal Christian Religion

In Kristín's story, her experience with the national church did little to introduce her to the Bible or to the gospel, and the same is true for most Icelanders. As surprising as it may seem, the Icelandic national church is one of the biggest barriers to the spread of the gospel in Iceland. Because organized Christianity is such a part of the fabric of Icelandic culture and tradition within the country, few Icelanders see the need to become converted or to live their lives dedicated to Jesus Christ as their Savior. They are already self-described Christians because of their culture; they are members of the national Lutheran church, and they've been baptized and confirmed to prove it.

If you think back to the history of Iceland, it should be no surprise that Icelanders keep their distance from Christianity. In 1000 A.D., Iceland's parliament decided to become Christians as long as they could continue pagan practices in the privacy of their homes. Similarly, during the Reformation, Iceland watched as the King of Denmark used Lutheranism to gain political power after a civil war. Now to be fair, a handful of Icelanders were transformed by the gospel, such as Hallgrímur Pétursson, who penned some of Iceland's most devotional hymns during the Reformation. However, Iceland's history with Christianity has been steeped in traditionalism and established religion, only to be accompanied by scarce spurts of revival and transformative faith.

Even worse, the national church has helped to facilitate the decline in morality and solid doctrine. Iceland has slowly declined into secularization since the late nineteenth and early twentieth century. According to Pétur Pétursson's Church and Social Change, the theological education in Iceland leaned toward Rationalism by the end of the 1800s and was managed and supported by the church.7 (If you recall from chapter 2, Rationalism is the philosophy that all of reality must be explained rationally.) Thus, the national Lutheran church has been teaching an anti-supernatural theology since the mid- to late-nineteenth century. By 1913, when a new law required that all officers in the church had to receive a degree from the University of Iceland, that only further cemented this belief system.[6]

To further complicate matters, the state pays all national Lutheran priests their salary. According to the *Reykjavík Grapevine*, one of Iceland's most well-known news magazines, the base salary per month in 2018 was 600,000 ISK, or approximately $4,800 USD. That is almost 200,000 ISK above the 2017 median salary in Iceland of 416,000 ISK—a large starting salary for Iceland, especially when that salary comes with additional perks.[8] Priests receive subsidized rent for their housing and are given the right to rent out church land to local farmers at a profit.[9] This makes becoming a Lutheran national priest a lucrative and desirable position in the Icelandic political and religious system.

Today, most priests within the national Lutheran church maintain a complex multiplicity of belief systems—rationalism, Christian heritage, and Icelandic tradition—without teaching core doctrines of the Christian faith. On the whole, national priests present the tradition of Christianity and couch faith in terms of good principles or moral lessons, without teaching the authority of Scripture or of Christ. Most are uncomfortable teaching about sin and avoid preaching the message that all must surrender and place their trust in Christ as Lord. As a whole, Iceland views national Lutheran priests more as agents of the state and Icelandic tradition than as ministers of Christ's grace and gospel.

Culturally, priests focused their work on major life events more than anything else: birth, coming of age, marriage, and death. At each point, the national church has some involvement in Icelanders' lives. Most children born in Iceland are baptized in the Lutheran church, at fourteen years old they are confirmed in the faith, many are married in the church, and finally, are buried. This traditional role of the church conveys Icelandic tradition more than it teaches Christian doctrine.

In the United States, confirmation or baptism usually involves a personal decision and is the first step to joining a local church. The confirmation or baptism class takes multiple hours or weeks to cover aspects of Christian doctrine specific to that church or denomination. This is nothing like confirmation in Iceland. In Iceland, nearly every teenager gets confirmed at 14—significantly motivated by the gifts they will receive at the afterparty (one Icelander estimated the value can be $3,000–$4,000 USD!). An Icelandic confirmation is more comparable to an elaborate sweet sixteen party or a quinceañera than it is to a religious practice.

The ceremony is so irreligious that even non-church organizations have started offering "confirmations." Take the Ethical Humanist Association, for example, which offers a civilian confirmation class that aims to "strengthen self-image, ambition, and a constructive attitude."[10] In this environment, what are teenagers confirmed into? The website continues: "The youth are strengthening their decision to be responsible citizens in a democratic society." While the class might be useful in a practical sense for teenagers to learn about contributing to Icelandic society, the original purpose of confirmation was to introduce Icelanders to the Christian faith. Now, the culture has gone so far as to take something that used to be fundamentally Christian and stripped it of its original meaning.

However, not surprisingly, the confirmation process within the national Lutheran church is not much better. Though classes will often include a few historical tidbits about Christianity, they often avoid biblical, doctrinally sound teachings about Jesus, the Bible, and salvation. In multiple interviews with Icelandic Christians, they described confirmation class as a "fun facts" version of Christianity. In one instance, a confirmation class included a worksheet where teens had to walk inside a church building to locate symbols on their worksheet, such as a shepherd's staff. The follow-up assignment matched the symbol with its historical meaning.

Whether Icelanders accept or reject the message of Christianity presented in confirmation class, they are responding to what is at best a watered-down representation of Christianity, and at worst a false one. Many Icelanders either think they are Christians or believe that Christianity cannot answer their deepest question, based on what the national Lutheran church teaches. Tragically, this presents a huge barrier for the spread of the gospel.

Guðrún Hrönn Jónsdóttir studied theology at the University of Iceland for her undergraduate degree because she wanted to serve as a deacon in the national church. Now a member of Lofstofan Baptistakirka, Guðrún told me about her experience over tea and biscuits at her home in a neighborhood just a few miles from downtown Reykjavík.

Soon after graduating from college, Guðrún attended a conference where many pastors from the national church presented, including one particularly memorable speaker. This national priest stood up and discounted the authority of Scripture and of Christ himself. Reflecting back on that presentation, Guðrún concluded: "To be honest the Jesus that she believes in is not the same Jesus that I believe in." Undervaluing the authority of Scripture is fairly common in Iceland, where "a lot of people just don't believe that things were exactly like the Bible says, even if they know some of the narrative of Jesus' life."

However, as nominal as many Icelandic Christians are, they still value the children's programming of local Icelandic churches. They offer a kind of Sunday school service that is geared toward children with games, some Bible stories, and an invitation for parents to participate. Unfortunately, Guðrún noted that these programs are more about games and activities than solid Christian teaching. "A lot of people in Iceland have the idea that if you are really Christian, then you are crazy," she said.[11]

And thus, generations of Icelanders have passed on "the form of godliness, but denying its power." Apart from the power of God, the national church holds significant sway over the hearts and minds of Icelanders. It will take a significant move of God's Spirit to call the Icelandic people back to himself in genuine faith, and for Icelanders to overcome the moralistic teachings presented by the national church to receive the transformative good news of Christ come to save sinners.

Barrier 3: Antagonism toward Christainity

To get to know some Icelanders and learn more about their approach to religion myself, I took an afternoon to speak with Icelanders in downtown Reykjavík on a casual Monday afternoon. Throngs of tourists had dwindled to a trickle by the afternoon, and I stepped into an art studio where I met **Sólveig Hólm**, a middle-aged Icelandic ceramics artist. Her crisp, arctic blue eyes penetrated into mine as we talked about art, creativity, inspiration, and faith.

Sólveig finds her inspiration for her melancholic figurines from the dark fairy tales of Hans Christian Andersen and the Grimm brothers. Many of these tales have been preserved in the Icelandic consciousness and she always found them inspiring. When I asked her about whether faith contributes to her inspiration, she said it did not. "For me, inspiration is connected to energy. Energy comes from the earth and connects every one of us."[12]

When I asked her about her personal faith, she identified as a Christian, but also expressed a fondness for Buddha and all religions. She views all religions as ultimately the same, but considers herself a Lutheran and attends services in the national church sporadically. The real benefit of the church, she said, is to counsel young couples before they get married. She believed the church was a good thing, but did not see any need to make Christianity central to her life.

In another art studio down the road, two artists in their young twenties did not identify with any religion, but instead viewed all religions as valid. One of the artists was a young man, whose grandfather was a priest in the Lutheran church, so he was very aware of what the national Lutheran church teaches. Ultimately, he rejected Christianity because he believes all religions exercise power over people and use shame to manipulate them. He was open to people having personal faith, and encouraged all people to decide what was meaningful for them, even saying he believed in a "presence" like God. Confirmed in the Lutheran faith as a teenager, this young artist did not remember if he was still a member of the national Lutheran church or not. Similarly the other artist, a young woman, believes that all people have something meaningful in their life that inspires them, but did not want to engage further on questions of her personal faith.

These stories of Icelanders illustrate the variety of approaches to Christianity and to religion in general within the country. While most Icelanders will know something *about* Christianity from confirmation class or from the heritage of previous generations, they are more likely to believe in a kind of "all roads lead to god" religious experience than they are to believe in Jesus Christ as their Lord and Savior.

As Icelandic culture has steadily shifted away from Christianity and biblical values over the past half-century, another vein of Icelanders have emerged: those antagonistic to the church. Where 50 years ago all Icelanders would have called themselves Christians, now you would find a number of Icelanders who are self-proclaimed atheists. While the entire country values the traditions that Christianity provides for the country, a growing number would not consider themselves Christians at all.

For those Icelanders who would call themselves atheists, their fight with Christianity is over socio-political issues, not primarily doubts in the existence of God. One of the first questions that Gunnar Gunnarsson receives when people discover he's a pastor who actually believes the Bible is this: "If God is a God of love, why does he hate homosexuals?" Almost as frequently, he gets questions like: "You don't *actually* believe that abortion is wrong, do you?" and finally, "Why would a good God allow such suffering in the world?"

Additionally, there is another form of atheism that has rejected Christianity simply because the church could not provide answers to their questions. The lack of strong theological teaching in Iceland has left State priests ill-equipped to answer these questions, and so Icelanders will largely keep their questions private.

Other forms of antagonism to Christianity have come not from atheists, but from a resurgence of the Old Norse religion. Called Ásatrú, this religion worships Þor (commonly spelled Thor), Loki, Óðinn, Týr, and the rest of the Nordic pantheon. The high priest of the religion, Hilmar Örn Hilmarsson, clarified the beliefs of the religion in an interview with *Iceland Magazine*. "I do not believe in a one-eyed man, riding an eight-legged horse," he said. "But the Poetic Edda is fundamentally about how life changes, and how you must be prepared to respond to the changes it brings."[13] In many ways, this resurgence of Old Norse religion recycles Iceland's values and cultural heritage.

Ásatrú is growing in popularity, as the largest non-Christian religion represented in Iceland with more than 4,000 members, or 1.25 percent of the population. By comparison, the Ethical Humanist Association, a self-proclaimed atheist group, has a membership of just 0.8 percent of the country. A still larger number of Icelanders fall into the "other" and "no religious organization" categories. The 2019 statistics for church and religious membership shows that 13 percent of the country identifies as "Other and not specified" and 7 percent identifies with "no religious organization." Together, that makes 20 percent of the country identifying with no religion at all.

And while on the streets of Reykjavík you are still more likely to find an Icelander who calls himself a Christian than an atheist, the number of self-proclaimed atheists is steadily increasing in Iceland. Over the next couple of decades, Iceland will face a crisis of culture. Without mature Christians within their society, Icelanders will have no foundation whereby they can call themselves a Christian country.

Barrier 4: Lack of Mature Christians

For faithful church member and Akureyri resident Kristín Gerðalíð, church consisted of six adults, most of whom were her uncles and extended family, gathering to take communion together. But that was irregular, and at the time I talked to her they had dwindled to taking communion together once every two weeks. The majority of their time spent together as a church was putting on a summer camp for children, where hundreds of kids learned about the Bible. A Brethren church founded by missionaries from the UK in the early 1900s, the church has gone from more than a hundred members to less than 10. With no pastor, there is no regular preaching of Scripture and the church itself is 'on life support.'

This lack of spiritual maturity has produced a chasm in this generation of Icelandic Christians. Those who are becoming saved are discipled by the few faithful followers in Christ around them. But outside of a handful of solid, Bible-preaching churches in Iceland, it is difficult to encounter the gospel in Iceland. Of course, God can use all means to communicate His good news to His children, but the reality remains that few pulpits preach the gospel in Iceland, and thus, few Icelanders have ever heard the truth of Christ and the gospel of salvation.

Furthermore, even strong and mature Christians carry the vestiges of the culture's approach to religion, and find it difficult to spread the gospel among family members, friends, and coworkers. That means that even among gospel-preaching churches, the gospel largely remains among the members of the congregation and is spreading at a snail's pace.

Conclusion

Truly, the spiritual landscape in Iceland is bleak. The darkness is palpable. The apathy is strong.

But praise be to God that though few lights for the gospel shine in Iceland, "the light shines in the darkness and the darkness has not overcome it" (John 1:5). By God's grace, there is hope for the church in Iceland, hope that is grounded in prayer and full of expectation at what God has already done and is doing in the church. The story of God's work now to spread the gospel in Iceland is full of His grace in the midst of suffering, faithfulness to His children, and calm assurance of salvation to those who believe.

The world needs more Icelandic Christians. And can you imagine what heaven will be like with more Icelandic Christians, praising God in Icelandic?

Perhaps God is using this little book to draw you, Reader, to make Jesus known in Iceland. I hope you keep that question in the back of your mind as you read the next chapter, for God is fully able to remove all these barriers to gospel progress with the power of His Word.

"Now to him who is able to keep you from stumbling and to present you blameless before the presence of His glory with great joy, to the only God, our Savior, through Jesus Christ our Lord, be glory, majesty, dominion, and authority, before all time and now and forever. Amen."
- Jude 24-25

5

THE FUTURE OF THE CHURCH IN ICELAND

"Iceland has 1,000 years of Christian heritage, and we want to redeem them. We want people to understand that these church buildings that are empty on Sundays aren't just museums of a time long past. They're not just a church organization funded by the government, but are houses of worship."

-Logan Douglas
Church planter in Iceland,
Redeemer City Church of Reykjavík

When you walk through downtown Reykjavík, you can't help but notice an imposing, glacier-like building that towers above the two- and three-story homes along the main thoroughfare, with its prism sharply contrasting the town's brightly colored street art. The building is Hallgrímskirkja (pronounced Hatl-greems-kirk-ya), Iceland's largest church building, and was built to mirror the glacial landscape surrounding it. Like shards of ice crystal, the church cuts through the skyline—there is no doubt it is the most impressive structure around. While the church holds services on Sundays, few attend and far more come just to take pictures.

Curious about what the church was *really* like, I decided to attend a Sunday service conducted in English. I walked in quietly, painfully conscious that I was late (parking was harder to find than I expected!). A deacon was standing in front of the door to ward off curious visitors, permitting only serious worshippers to enter. I grabbed a program and settled into a mossy green pew, close to the rear of the room.

As a follower of Christ, I tuned in for any glimpse of the gospel in the service. What I found was both surprising and concerning. Little gems of the gospel were tucked away in elements of the liturgy such as these phrases: "For the sake of your Son Jesus Christ, who died for us, forgive us all that is past and grant that we may serve you," and "We do not presume to come to this your table, merciful Lord, trusting in our own righteousness, but in your manifold and great mercies."[1] The recitation of the Nicene Creed corporately refreshed my heart as I reminded myself of the truth of God's Word and of His Son, Jesus Christ our Lord.

In the middle of the service, a distinct shift occurred after the priest presented his homily. In his exposition of Luke 9, the passage where a man asks Jesus if he could go and bury his father before following Christ, Vicar Bjarni Þór Bjarnason stated the call of discipleship is simple. "Jesus promises to help us," he said, "To follow the call of discipleship, which is to be called a Christian where you are, in your profession."

He concluded his homily and transitioned to communion. In this service, communion was open to everyone, with no limits. All were welcome to "eat the body and blood of Christ" without a mention of repentance from sin, rather the priest focused on how communion provides peace.

The conflicted message I experienced in the service concerned me, so I found Vicar Bjarni afterward and asked him to clarify the gospel and the core message of Christianity. His response was, "Love God and love your neighbor. That's it." Next to him, sitting at a table with her coffee and the remnant of a doughnut in front of her, a woman agreed. Her husband identifies as an atheist, but she considered him an agnostic

---

[1] Since the service I attended was entirely in English, the liturgy was taken from the Anglican *Book of Common Prayer*.

because he *tries to do something good for someone else every day.* Not only did the vicar agree with her, but he said the man was a Christian. Vicar Bjarni continued, saying that "we can never say whether someone is a Christian, only God can do that."

I was a bit puzzled by this interaction, and so I asked him for more clarification. "If Christianity is all about loving your neighbor, why did Christ die?" I asked. He said the gospel is the message that God decided to send his Son, Jesus, who was crucified and resurrected: "Jesus died to reconcile us, to die for our sins." But when I asked what sin was, he said that "sin is when there is a gap between God and man. Jesus bridges that gap."[2]

So while Vicar Bjarni expressed elements of the gospel, in a few key areas he comfortably slid into an all-inclusive religiosity that promises love for everyone, salvation for anyone who loves their neighbor and calls themselves a Christian, and offers a message of love and peace. Some aspects of that message are genuinely good and reflect pieces of the gospel, however, overall it lacked the core truth of "repent and believe the good news" (Mark 1:15) that John the Baptist proclaimed as he prepared the way for our Savior, Jesus Christ.

This story illustrates the current state of the church in Iceland. Hallgrímskirkja is far from the only Icelandic church struggling to fill the pews on Sundays. While their heritage of Christian doctrine may contain elements of the gospel, a select few believe it at face value and live transformed lives.

So what is next for Christianity in Iceland? In a country filled with individuals who respond to religion with apathy, is there any hope for Christian revival? Honestly, apart from the work of God in Iceland, no. There is no human strategy that will reverse Iceland's slide into irreligious pluralism.

The future of the church in Iceland looks bleak, given the current culture, and Icelandic Christians are in great need for prayer, encouragement, and support. And yet, the work of God is not about strategies, support, or human effort. It *is* about Jesus and making Him known, and that is a work that only God can accomplish through the Holy Spirit. Without the Spirit working in someone's life, it is more impossible for them to come to faith in Christ than it is for a camel to squeeze itself through the eye of a needle. As Jesus exhorted his disciples, "with man this is impossible, but with God all things are possible" (Matt. 19:25-26).

1. The Church on the Brink

The reality is that very few Icelanders attend church regularly, and even fewer hear the gospel preached regularly from their pulpits. Within Iceland's population of 365,000, somewhere between 0.2–2 percent of church members attend any church.[3] That works out to a few thousand Icelanders sitting in church pews on an average Sunday.

Even more stark than that is the number of gospel-preaching churches in Iceland. Gunnar Gunnarsson, pastor of Loftstofan Baptistakirkja, counted on two hands the number of churches that he knew regularly preached the gospel of sin, repentance, and God's salvation through Christ. Even being generous with attendance numbers, those churches minister to about 500 people on a Sunday. That's 0.14 percent of the entire country's population!

In addition, access to Bibles and biblical theology books written in Icelandic is at an all-time low. The last Christian publishing house in Iceland closed in the 1960s and no other company has replaced it. While Gunnar has worked independently to translate devotional and theological articles into Icelandic, the reality is that half a century has passed since Icelanders have had an older generation passing down the lessons God has been teaching them through the written word.

Further, because books are so expensive in Iceland, it is difficult for Icelanders to afford a personal copy of the Bible. A budget edition of the Bible in Icelandic costs about 5500 Icelandic Krona, or approximately $40 USD, at the University of Iceland bookstore. Even if you can obtain an Icelandic Bible for yourself, a number of translations have some controversy over the accuracy of the translation. English Bibles are no better and are similarly expensive to buy and difficult to find. Overall, obtaining a Bible in Iceland, whether translated into Icelandic or English, is difficult and expensive—and even if you find one it may not be a faithful translation of the text.

The lack of access to Scripture, books on Christian living, and fellow Christians who are committed to their faith has greatly affected the current spiritual landscape in Iceland. With few elders and older believers to shepherd and teach, the church suffers from the lack of spiritual leadership from senior generations. Without a body of believers filled with *both* mature believers *and* new converts, pastors bear the brunt of spiritual leadership—not ideal for the long term health of the church in Iceland.

For those pastors, and for anyone who is interested in theological studies in Iceland, the options for seminary training are few and far between. The only seminary in the country is run by the University of Iceland and focuses on training priests for the state-run Lutheran church. For pastors to receive gospel-centered seminary training, they must leave their beloved country for a seminary in another country.

Those who attend the University's seminary typically do so because they are interested in a stable government job, not because they are interested in learning more about God or His Word. And the state-run seminary does little to encourage vibrant faith. Quite the opposite, the state-run seminary uses popular theology books to discredit the authority and veracity of the Word of God.

Take for example the first day of class at the University. Pastor Gunnar Gunnarson's wife, Svava Ómarsdóttir, decided to enroll in some theology classes to see if she could learn more about God and theology. On the first day of class in a room surrounded by theology students at the University of Iceland, Svava watched as her classmates answered the question:

"Why are you studying theology?"

As a pastor's wife and committed Christian, Svava shared that she was there to learn more about God and learn how to articulate theology to others.

But as classmates completed the circle in answer to the question, almost every one revealed that by becoming a priest they were guaranteed a government job and came to seminary to pursue theology as a career. Only one broke the trend: she wanted to be the first lesbian priest ordained in the State Lutheran Church.

And yet, not all priests in the State Lutheran Church are bereft of the gospel—in fact, I met with a priest named Kjartan Jónsson who clearly articulated the gospel and his desire to disciple others in the faith. As a young man, Kjartan came to faith through the ministry of the YMCA before he graduated from the state-run seminary and worked as a missionary in Africa for 20 years. After returning to Iceland in the early 2000s, Kjartan became a priest in the State Church and has since started a Bible study called SALT for those who want to dig into Scripture and Christianity.

His heart is to reach this generation of Icelanders with the gospel, and to find the "key to their heart." Willing to change elements of the service to attract younger generations, he also offers Christianity 101 classes called "Alpha Classes" to teach core tenets of Christianity. When I asked him about his hope for the future, he was not optimistic. "Some say the state church will crumble," he said. "The younger generation is losing their Christian heritage. If the chain breaks, it will be in this generation."

Kjartan was fixed in his resolve to preach the gospel without compromise, even if it does not attract younger people. "We don't change the gospel; it is final," he said. "It is important that we are not ashamed. This is the basis of the church."[4]

While Kjartan and other pastors like him work to attract young people to join the church, there is a palpable lack of gospel-centered teaching in the vast majority of national Lutheran churches, and there are simply not enough churches that can fill the void.

One of the greatest needs of the church in Iceland today

is for more gospel-centered believers to join gospel-centered churches, and live in such a way to proclaim Christ throughout the country. With the current statistics, a shockingly few number of Icelanders are part of a gospel-centered church. It's time to reverse the trend.

2. Needed: A Vision of Growth in Christ

Since the year 1000, Iceland has had a complicated relationship with Christianity and most Icelanders are living with the consequences today. Because Iceland has largely continued practicing the same traditional Lutheranism, Icelanders have no context to imagine Iceland any different than it is today. It takes a significant working of God through his Holy Spirit to open hearts hardened by decades of apathy.

The question then presents itself, "what would it look like for Iceland to be filled with a family of God growing in Christ-likeness?"

First and foremost, faithful Christians and churches in Iceland must rediscover the joy of the Lord that is their strength, the beauty of the good news in Christ, and the hope found in eternal life through Jesus Christ the Lord. Only a handful of churches preach these simple, life-transformative truths to a few hundred faithful Icelanders in the entire country. For gospel-centered Christians to grow within this island nation, the body of Christ must be encouraged to embrace a life of Christlikeness, and catch a vision of what sacrifice looks like in mundane, day-to-day faithfulness.

In every culture, Christlikeness is counter-cultural. There's a reason that Paul calls every church "saints" in his letters to them. The word saint translates "set-apart ones" or "holy ones." Iceland is no different, and aspects of Icelandic culture clash with becoming "little Christs" or *Christ-ians*.

Most apparent is the moral apathy in Iceland. Due to the cultural apathy regarding Christianity, most Icelanders grow up with few notions of living in accordance with Scripture. Not only is the culture permissive when it comes to morality, but a pervasive acceptance of "all religions lead to god" is present in the society. Thus, their religion and lifestyle are kept distinct and separate.

That in itself is a very human problem! All of us tend to place our lifestyle ahead of living like Christ. How often have I taken my morning to scroll through Instagram instead of talk to God? How often have I harbored sin and self-righteously judged that "I'm not like *those people*" in the same spirit as the Prodigal Son's older brother? How many times have I told God that I would run my life much better than Him, thank you very much?

The same struggle is present within Icelandic society, where it is difficult to live as a counter-cultural, faithful Christians. The gospel must be central in each of our lives as Christians, whatever cultural tendencies we bring to the table. Gospel-preaching churches must continue to present the message of "living for Christ" so that new believers can become discipled and begin to live according to the Scriptures. Biblical discipleship in Iceland requires a strong foundation in all areas, but particularly in developing an understanding of Scripture and of biblical theology.

Since the national Lutheran church is so involved in children's programs and confirmations, many Icelanders have a limited notion of what Christianity is, having never read the Bible for themselves. Thus, new believers in gospel-preaching churches in Iceland begin with little Bible knowledge and are like "newborn infants, and long for the pure spiritual milk, that by it they may grow up into salvation." (1 Pet. 2:2) For the first time in their lives, they experience Scripture as the Word of God. So while there is a great need for the gospel to be spread, there is an equally great need for gospel-preaching churches to equip believers with solid Scriptural teaching.

Furthermore, still other independent Icelandic churches are teaching extra-biblical theology. Especially among a handful of independent churches, a variety of heterodoxical theologies may be present. Take for example One-ness Theology, which teaches that Jesus is the only person of the Trinity, or Word of Faith teaching, which can be found among the prosperity gospel movement. These churches may express aspects of the gospel, but their picture is tainted by other beliefs that present another gospel.

However, there is still grace present in these partial presentations of the gospel, even distorted by false theologies. From the personal testimonies of four of the original members of Loftstofan—Gunnar, Svava, Kristín, and her husband, Friðberg—some of these very churches awakened their hearts to the idea that God is a real person, that Jesus saves, and that Jesus is worth sacrificing their lives. Though the teaching they received did not include teaching about how they should live in Christ after receiving him, they did receive the basic message of repentance and faith. These churches are presenting the gospel, and we should pray that they deepen the message to present an even clearer call to live for Christ.

Finally, for the church in Iceland to grow in Christlikeness, the members of the church must be equipped to share the gospel with friends and family members, to "give a defense for the hope that lies within them" (1 Pet. 3:15).

If you recall from the previous chapter, Kristín Björg Karlsdóttir said that her parents still do not grasp that she *really* believes the Bible is the Word of God and that Jesus is the Son of God. This overwhelming response of incredulity to Christ-followers makes it difficult to share the gospel.

Other Icelanders may respond to the gospel with fierce questioning. "Why did God command the Israelites to wipe out entire people groups?" "If God is love, why does he hate homosexuals?" "Are you telling me that God cares who I sleep with?" These questions and more often come up in conversation once a believer begins to share the gospel. And while not every member needs to be the next Ravi Zacharias in their level of apologetics training, an ability to respond to questions with grace and truth is necessary for the gospel to take hold in the hearts and minds of fellow Icelanders.

The challenges for the church in Iceland are not unlike the challenges for the church universal. And yet, the challenges of apathy, religious complacency, and growing antagonism toward Christ mark the unique manifestation of those challenges in Iceland today.

3. Hope remains, the gospel will go forth

When looking ahead, the future of the church in Iceland is uncertain. With so few Christians attending church and even fewer attending gospel-centered churches, it looks as though Christ has lost his influence in Iceland. However, the gospel *is* spreading in Iceland, and while there is much work left to be done, faithful followers of Christ are boldly proclaiming the truth.

Through faithful evangelism, Loftstofan Baptistakirkja has seen individuals come to dedicate their lives to Christ. This past year, a few individuals were baptized, bringing the church membership up to a few dozen. Prayerfully, that number will grow as more converts receive the grace of Christ.

Since its founding, Loftstofan has made concerted efforts to reach the local community and the local university's college students. Through an active campus ministry and regular events, college students visit Loftstofan to learn more. In addition, Loftstofan has begun a number of regular ministries to the surrounding community, and has seen relationships continue to grow.

Beyond Loftstofan, new churches are beginning to take root as well. Logan and Carla Douglas moved to Reykjavík in April 2019 to begin church planting efforts for an English-speaking church in Reykjavík called *Redeemer City Church of Reykjavík*. Logan and Carla started their work in Iceland by joining Loftstofan for their first year to become familiar with the culture and to establish themselves before they branch off and begin a church in the heart of Reykjavík in 2020.

Another expression of gospel ministry is within pentecostal churches in Iceland, loosely similar to Assembly of God churches in the United States. Churches within that denomination include Hvítasunnukirkjan Fíladelfía (Brotherly Love Pentecostal Church), and a handful of church plant congregations around the country. They also express a vibrant and personal faith that is lived in practice, as well as in preaching.

Still other churches, such as the Icelandic House of

Prayer, First Baptist Church of Keflavík, and various Pente-costal churches are also stewards of God's grace. In various ways, these churches are preaching the gospel and calling Christians to live like Christ.

Finally, Christians around the world are praying for church plants that have not yet begun! Christians from Asia, the Middle East, Europe, Africa, and the Americas are praying for Iceland, and a number are considering moving to Iceland permanently to support the ministry. Pastor Gunnar Gunnar-son is encouraged by people praying for Iceland, and for those from both within Iceland and without who want to raise up a harvest, disciple others, and "hold to the Word whatever the cost may be to following Christ in this country." He added, "I'm excited to see what God will do with unimpressive peo-ple to do hopefully impressive things to give him the glory."[5]

Prayers for a church plant in Akureyri, Iceland's sec-ond-largest city, have been ongoing for the past several years, spearheaded by Veritas City Church in Georgetown, Virginia, and Redemption Church in Maryland. Both of these Ameri-can churches have partnered with Loftstofan and Redeemer City Church of Reykjavík to consider how best to engage with church planting in Akureyri.

Ministry to college students in Akureyri is also growing through the ministry of Kristín Gerðalíð, who has joined with Agape (Campus Crusade's international branch) to begin an evangelism ministry to the university in town. These minis-tries are just beginning, so much prayer is needed for them to grow and flourish through the faithful teaching of God's Word and encouragement of his saints.

Churches in the U.S., Canada, and the U.K. have partnered with churches in Iceland to send short term missions teams to support discipleship and theological training efforts in Ice-land. From Pillar Church of Dumfries, Virginia, USA, to Église du Plateau in Montreal, Canada, groups have come to encour-age and support the work of gospel-preaching churches in the Iceland Project network and have encouraged the mem-bers of those churches as a whole.

And yet, there is a lot of work to be done in sharing the

gospel with Icelanders. Loftstofan church member Guðrun Hrönn Jónsdóttir expressed both discouragement and hope as she considered preaching the gospel with her friends, family, and neighbors. "Often I have been discouraged thinking there is no way for Icelanders to join our church, but then I remind myself that it's our job to sow the seed and we don't always know what kind of soil the seed falls into. But if we don't sow any seeds, then nothing will grow out of it."[6]

4. God's Word does not return void

Church attendance is in decline. A growing number of Icelanders are declaring themselves atheists. Numerous Icelanders are so apathetic that they claim no religion. The future of the church in Iceland is in a tenuous position. Without a generation of believers transformed by the gospel, Iceland has little hope of remaining a Christian nation in the next 50 years. State churches are not garnering enough attendance to be self-sustaining. And with so many millennial Icelanders leaving the church and declaring themselves non-religious, that trend is unlikely to reverse anytime soon.

"But God."

Those are two of the most transformational words in all of Scripture, and they apply here. *But God* is at work in Iceland, drawing Icelanders to himself by the faithful preaching of His Word. It is the "power of God unto salvation for those who believe." (Rom. 1:16) A work of this magnitude could not be completed by human effort alone, but by the grace of God.

So we pray. We hope. We work. We believe that one day, we will join with our Icelandic brothers and sisters of the faith—united by the good news and freedom we have found in Christ. Though not the present reality of Iceland, there is great hope that one day Iceland will bring forth many courageous and faithful servants of the King of Kings.

They will join with the saints already serving in Iceland—men and women such as Gunnar and Svava, Logan and Carla,

Helgi and Aron (pastors at Fíladelfía), and others who have dedicated their lives to the work of proclaiming God's Word among the people of Iceland. This is no task for the faint of heart, but it is a task for those willing to press into the grace of Christ and intercede on behalf of those whom God is calling to Himself.

Will you join them? Perhaps you are part of the story of God's work in Iceland. Perhaps God is calling you to sacrifice for the sake of the gospel in Iceland. Perhaps God is calling you to go and make disciples in Iceland.

6

HOW CAN YOU HELP

"Jesus' disciples went all over the world sharing this gospel. That's what I want to see in our church. I want to see a church that is growing inward, outward, and upward—in community and love for one another, in love for God, and in love for others in the community."

-Gunnar Gunnarsson
Pastor and Church Planter,
Loftstofan Baptistakirkja in Reykjavik

The ministry work in Iceland is daunting. After decades of the state church preaching a watered-down gospel, the majority of Icelanders associate Christianity with Icelandic tradition and not with the freedom found when Christ delivers sinners. Today, few Icelanders are equipped and able to take up the mantle and preach the message of grace.

Apart from the grace of Christ, there are so few Icelanders to pass on the faith that Christianity could die out completely in the next 50 years. Unless the body of Christ hears the call and takes the message of Christ to the people of Iceland, there is little hope for revival and freedom among the Icelandic people.

If you feel any tug of God's Spirit on your heart, I encourage you to commit yourself to join the ministry in Iceland. Reading this book is a great start! And beyond that, there are so many ways you can get involved. Consider incorporating one or more of the following ways to support the ministry in

Iceland. Most importantly, like any move of God's Spirit, the first step is to commit to prayer.

1. Commit to Pray

God's work is often preceded by prayer, and the same is true in Iceland. Prayer for the church, the ministry, the country, and the spread of the gospel here is desperately needed.

Starting with prayer is modeled by the early church. Prayer was so immediate that Jesus' disciples returned from Jesus' resurrection on the Mount of Olives and dedicated themselves to pray. (Acts 1:14) In the earliest days of the church, we see a model of Christ forming a new church. First, the believers faithfully unite together to pray. Then, they appoint church leadership. After that, the church faithfully gathers together at Pentecost and the Holy Spirit comes upon the church, emboldening them to preach the gospel to the lost.

This work of the early church in Acts is a picture of God's work among his people to draw many to himself:

1. Prayer & Fasting
2. Elders are appointed
3. The Holy Spirit emboldens Christians to reach others with the gospel.

The same applies here! For ministry in Iceland to flourish, we must first unite together in prayer "for apart from him we can do nothing." (John 15:5)

I recently heard a sermon by a pastor[1] who is ministering the gospel in the Middle East. He asked my local church: If you had all the resources available to you—a ginormous financial budget for missions, a constant supply of people willing to go on teams, and the best missions strategies around—would you be equipped to support God's work to plant churches in other places?

As members of a new church plant ourselves, we nodded along from our foldable Costco plastic chairs, excited about this vision of planting churches in the future. "Prayer," he con-

---

[1] Name protected for safety.

tinued," is the single most valuable resource you have to participate in God's work to save the lost."

By committing to pray, you are joining fellow Christians who have been interceding for decades, petitioning God to work in Iceland. Take Veronika Kolomichuk for example. She is the daughter of an American military man and Icelandic mother who was born and raised in Iceland, but came to faith in the United States in the 1980s. She was just 20 years old when she first came to know Christ as her Savior, and always had a desire to go back and visit her mother's country. In 2000, she finally got the chance to visit Iceland and was struck by the palpable spiritual darkness. Since then, Veronika has committed to pray for her family in Iceland to be saved, and for the country as a whole to experience a revival of the gospel.

Her ministry to steadfastly pray came with many discouraging years where it seemed like God did not hear her prayers, and she despaired that "God had abandoned the Icelandic people." Yet, she faithfully prayed that God would bring revival and spread the gospel among the Icelanders. After her visit in 2000 gave her a renewed sense of the spiritual darkness in Iceland, she continued to pray. After years of praying for Iceland, Veronika shared her burden for the country in the women's Bible study at her church. Through a string of seemingly unrelated coincidences, one of the ladies in her Bible study introduced her to something they called "the Iceland Project," run at that time by Stafford Baptist Church in Stafford, Virginia.

That original Iceland Project began when pastor Bill Jessup, the pastor of Stafford Baptist Church, responded to God's call to pray for Iceland. He shared his heart to pray for the country with the church and staff, and they decided to rotate staff members for three months at a time at a Reykjavík apartment starting in 2005. After a few years of prayer but little headway, Colby and Annie Garman, who were on staff at Stafford, moved to Iceland long-term and lived in Reykjavík for about three years. A medical emergency with one of the Garman's children called them back unexpectedly to the United States.

Around that same time, Gunnar Gunnarsson, who was working simultaneously as a grocery store clerk and layman pastor, had discovered while listening to a church planting podcast that a church in Virginia was looking for an Icelander to plant a church in Iceland. Through that chance comment on a podcast, Gunnar connected with Stafford Baptist Church, where he began to learn from pastors in the United States and deepened his walk with Christ. Eventually, that effort gave Gunnar resources to mature the church he had just planted, called Loftstofan Baptistakirkja, which translated means "Upper Room Baptist Church."

"I started praying for this country, feeling like God had forgotten them. And God showed me how much he cares and that he's moving people," Veronika concluded, as she recounted the story to me. Over the course of 10 years, Veronika went from being prompted by God to pray for the people in Iceland to watching as God answered her prayer in the form of a fledgling church. Loftstofan Baptistakirkja is just one of God's answers to her prayers. For Veronika, she intends to make her commitment to pray for Iceland lifelong. Her goal is to learn enough of the Icelandic language to share the gospel with her mother's family and hopes to see them come to faith in Christ.[2]

Veronika Kolomichuk is just one example of the faithful believers who have dedicated years of their lives to pray for God to spread His good news through the *Land of Fire and Ice*. Colby Garman and his wife, Annie, prayed alongside that early team of believers who went to Iceland to pray. In the years the Garmans spent in Iceland, they invited countless Icelanders over to their home, all the while faithfully praying that God would save some. In the end, their ministry was one of plowing the field and sowing the seeds that are now bearing fruit in Icelandic churches and the Iceland Project as a whole. God is "providing the increase" as He did in the Corinthian church. (1 Cor. 3:6)

And now, God continues to answer the steadfast prayers of Gunnar Gunnarsson and the members of Loftstofan Baptistakirkja—that God would raise up more faithful believers within Iceland, that he would draw many to himself, and that he would plant many more churches in Iceland. Redeemer City Church, planted by Logan Douglas and his wife, Carla, is one answer to that prayer. Only God knows who else will be an answer to those prayers. Perhaps you are one of them?

For specific prayer requests in a detailed prayer guide, please see the end of this chapter.

2. Come and See what God is doing in Iceland

The ministry needs in Iceland are numerous, so any faithful member of Christ's body is able to serve the church in Iceland. No matter what your gifts may be, come and see what God is doing in Iceland! Your time and effort would be a great help to the church here. Christ's words ring out like a call to Iceland, "the harvest is plentiful but the laborers are few." (Matt. 9:37) There is a great need for believers to partner with the Icelandic church and catch the vision that Christ would be made known in Iceland.

Start by coming for a **vision trip** to connect with faithful churches in Iceland and see what God is doing among His followers in Iceland. A one-week vision trip is a great way to get a taste of the needs of the ministry in churches connected to the Iceland Project. Come with your hearts open to the Lord's guiding and directing, and consider what God might call you to do after you return to your own church. Perhaps you commit to pray. Perhaps you commit to support financially or to send teams who encourage the brothers and sisters in Iceland. No matter the specific outcome from a vision trip, the purpose is to introduce the needs of the church in Iceland and to allow you the chance to see what God is doing among his people.

Because of the challenges of building relationships with Icelanders, most of the ministry in Iceland is the result of years of faithful, prayerful, and steadfast work. If you are sensing God calling you to work in the ministry in Iceland, **consider moving to Iceland for 1–3 years** and plant yourself in one of the local gospel-preaching churches.

One of the easiest ways to obtain a visa to live in Iceland for a few years is through education. As a socialist-leaning European country, Iceland heavily subsidizes their education. Thus, one year of tuition at the University of Iceland costs the equivalent of $700 USD. That's the same price as a round trip plane ticket! If you are planning to get a Bachelor's degree or Master's degree in the next few years and you believe the Lord is calling you to Iceland, consider getting your degree in Iceland instead! The University offers degrees in English in a variety of subjects, including degrees in the Icelandic language, so you can converse in Icelandic while ministering to the church in Iceland.

While in Iceland, consider joining one of the college ministries run by a gospel-preaching church, or join in an official capacity as part of the **College Intern Program** run by Logan Douglas out of Redeemer City Church of Reykjavík.[2] Simply follow the process of applying to the University of Iceland and then follow the process to apply for a visa. Additionally, reach out to the churches in Iceland to consider what time would best serve them and plan accordingly. If God is calling you to live in Iceland, this might be one avenue that would allow you to do what He has called you to pursue!

Want to support the church in Iceland to an even greater degree? Consider making a **lifetime commitment** to live in Iceland. Building trust among Icelanders as friends is vital to the spread of the gospel and vital to their growth in Christ as disciples. If you sense God's calling to Iceland, would you consider living in Iceland indefinitely?

In Iceland, the ministry needs are great and there are numerous ways to get involved. If you have gifting in media, video, or photography, you can put those skills to use by supporting the ministry team by editing videos, shooting new footage, or brainstorming new projects. If you are skilled in theological training and discipleship, you can join opportuni-

---

[2] Logan Douglas's contact information is provided in the Resources section at the end of this book.

ties to come for a week and support training and discipleship of church members. And finally, if your gift is in encouragement, consider a trip simply to encourage the pastors and members of the churches in Iceland. Many fight isolation daily as a true follower of Christ, so coming with the heart to encourage can make a big difference! By simply coming to see what God is doing in Iceland, you will provide encouragement and support to God's people in Iceland. What are you waiting for?!

If a move to Iceland or extended visit is outside the realm of possibility for you, consider supporting the ministry in Iceland by sending others from your church to Iceland. To get started, subscribe to email updates on the Iceland Project website (www.theIcelandProject.org).

3. Support the Ministry

Ministering the gospel in Iceland is a significant challenge in numerous ways. One specific challenge extends to financial hardships. Not only is the work in Iceland hard, between evangelism and discipleship within the congregation, but there are few church members to support their pastors.

Furthermore, because of the complicated relationship between church and state, the Icelandic government uses tax dollars to support the priests and pastors of churches. For this reason, Icelandic church members assume that their pastors will be supported by the state, thinking "my taxes support the church." This means that few Icelandic believers are in the habit of sacrificially giving to their churches. According to Gunnar Gunnarsson, that makes it very difficult to make a church plant self-sustaining and estimates it takes approximately 10 years for a church to be self-sufficient financially. By comparison, most church planting financial models expect church plants in the United States to be self-sufficient in 3-5 years.

The cost of living in Iceland only adds to the challenge. Income taxes in Iceland hover at 46.24 percent, and do not take additional sales or gas taxes into consideration.[3] Food prices are also inflated, since many items are imported and taxed at a premium. In a word, Iceland is an *expensive* place to live.

To support themselves, most adults combine incomes in a two-partner household to support the needs of their family, and may even work multiple jobs. For the pastors who are dedicating their lives to serve the church, they have very little additional time to support their own families. As a result, in order to give the proper time to shepherding their flock, pastors in Iceland must sacrifice income opportunities to care for their churches *and* support their families.

Would you consider contributing financially so that gospel workers can focus on the ministry at hand? As Paul reminds us in 1 Timothy 5:17-18, "Let the elders who rule well be considered worthy of double honor, especially those who labor in preaching and teaching. For the Scripture says, 'You shall not muzzle an ox when it treads out the grain,' and, 'The laborer deserves his wages.'" Certainly, shepherds of the church in Iceland deserve their wages, and you can be part of their ministry by supporting them financially.

4. Spread the word!

Given the enormous needs of the church in Iceland and the sheer lack of mature believers in the country, there are also few people to share ministry needs with others. You can be a part of that ministry to spread the word! If God has laid this ministry on your heart, freely share it with others. When Christian brothers and sisters bring up Iceland in conversation, share with them the needs of the church.

Sign up for email updates from The Iceland Project and forward them to friends and loved ones. Pass along the needs in Iceland to your pastors, small group leaders, and members of your church. Connect with believers at other local churches and share the needs and prayer requests with them. Most importantly, commit to pray regularly that the gospel would spread in Iceland and ask God to direct you to share with others. He will show you the people and give you the words to speak, as Jesus promises in Matthew, "Go therefore and make disciples of all nations, baptizing them in the name of the Father and of the Son and of the Holy Spirit, teaching them to observe all that I have commanded you. And behold, I am with you always, to the end of the age." (Matt 28:19-20)

The book you are holding in your hands is also a great tool. After you have finished reading it, consider giving your copy to a friend, pastor, or fellow believer. The needs are great, and the more people who know about the needs of the church, the more people can pray and join the ministry!

There are also a number of excellent media resources. The Iceland Project documentary, *Christian by Default*, paints an accurate picture of the state of the church in Iceland and provides the perfect introduction for anyone who might be interested in the ministry in Iceland. Other video and book resources are available in the Additional Resources and Sources sections at the back of this book, so take a look and spread the word!

5. Final Words

Jesus' words ring out among the fjords and glaciers, in empty pews and down tourist-thronged streets in Reykjavík, "the harvest is plentiful but the laborers are few" (Matt. 9:37). Who will go and preach the good news of repentance and faith in Christ? Who will proclaim God's Word to a country steeped in the appearance of godliness, while denying its power? Perhaps that's you.

God is certainly at work among the Icelandic people, drawing them closer to himself through the faithful witness of a remnant of believers, but they need support and encouragement. Paul needed his faithful friend and encourager, Barnabas, so the shepherds of the church in Iceland need friends and encouragers. The early church needed Aquila and Priscilla to join their endeavors as a husband and wife duo, so the church in Iceland also needs faithful husband and wife duos to display the gospel through their marriage. Furthermore, as Timothy, with all his youthful enthusiasm, joined wholeheartedly in Paul's ministry, so the church in Iceland needs young single men and women who are dedicated to discipleship and willing to become faithful servant leaders of the next generation.

Do you sense the call of the Lord to get involved in Iceland for His glory? Then come on in! The water's fine! You will become a part of the work God is doing to preserve a remnant of the gospel for future generations in this beautiful island. Without Him working, there is little hope for the future of the church in Iceland, but with the help of the Holy Spirit, nothing is impossible. Thanks be to God!

We pray for a future far different than the current reality in Iceland—a future where churches are full of believers of every age, discipling one another to become more like Jesus Christ each day. Imagine the sheer joy overflowing from the church as believers rejoice anew in the goodness of the Lord given through his Son, Jesus Christ. Imagine believers growing more and more like Christ, growing in maturity, and elders (who once were addicted, broken, shattered, atheists, hopeless, sinners) now shepherd the flock with grace and wisdom. A family community grows, much like that of the early church, and believers come to find their church is their *spiritual family*.

As the church grows in maturity, the household of God overflows in ministry to others. College ministry flourishes and the young people who are searching for answers in everything from alcohol and sex, to self-image and false religions, turn away from those things and believe in Jesus Christ as their Lord and Savior. The churches in Iceland work together to minister to the poor, abandoned, homeless, and addicted—showing them the mercy of our Lord to use the foolish things of the world to shame the wise. Evangelism efforts grow as mature believers share the gospel with their family, friends, and neighbors.

Eventually the church grows strong enough to support a seminary, publishing house, counseling ministries, and multi-generational discipleship. Spiritual grandchildren of this current generation build up the church to always point back to Christ. And in all, this creative, bold, joy-filled church grows in excitement to share the love of Christ with the rest of the world. It's a great work, so beyond human capacity. But thank God! We serve One who is able to do "far more abundantly above what we could ask or think." (Eph 3:20)

What more are you waiting for?

God is faithful to work His will in the earth and to build up His bride, the church, to proclaim His good news to the end of the world. God loves the Icelandic people, knows their hearts, and earnestly desires them to know Him. Thank God that his vision for the Icelandic people is redemptive, and He will complete the work that he has begun in Iceland.

> *Now to Him who is able to do far more abundantly than all that we ask or think, according to the power at work within us, to Him be glory in the church and in Christ Jesus throughout all generations, forever and ever. Amen."*
> -Ephesians 3:20-21

PRAYER GUIDE FOR ICELAND

1. For the Equipping of the Saints

- **Faithful Workers** - First and foremost, pray for faithful workers of the gospel to lead the ministry in Iceland, "holding firm to the trustworthy Word." (Tit. 1:9) Iceland needs faithful ministers of the gospel, faithful shepherds, and faithful teachers of the Word of God.

- **Discipleship** - Given the lack of mature believers in Iceland, there is an incredible lack of discipleship. Pray that God would raise up mature believers in Christ and equip them to replicate themselves in others.

- **Theological depth and maturity** - The only seminary in Iceland is run by the state, and has long since left the true gospel behind. Pray that God would provide resources to the Icelandic people in their language to encourage them in the faith and to train them in the richness of God's Word. Pray also for Icelandic pastors to be trained and equipped.

- **Encouragement** - Living in a country with so few faithful believers can be isolating and challenging for many. Pray that God would encourage and comfort His people by His Spirit and send faithful believers to partner with them for the spread of the gospel. Like Barnabas, Aquila, and Priscila encouraged Paul, pray for God to raise up encouragers to support those faithfully spreading the gospel and preaching His Word in Iceland.

2. For the Gospel to go forth

- **The Spread of the Gospel** - With a people that traditionally considers themselves Christians, many Icelanders are unaware of the gospel. Pray that in the midst of such spiritual apathy, faithful followers of Christ would have the boldness to proclaim their faith to their friends, coworkers, and family members—to the point of being ridiculed for being a zealous Christian.

- **For God to break down Walls of Apathy** - Many in Iceland would not consider themselves religious at all, and spend most of their lives in a haze of apathy. Pray that God would break through this wall of apathy and shine His light of grace.

- **Repentance and Faith** - Pray that the people of Iceland would not be willing to settle for a life of self-reliance, but would be willing to repent and receive God's transformative grace.

- **Healing from Brokenness** - Alcoholism, additions, and broken homes are commonplace in Iceland. Pray that God would heal brokeness and redeem anyone who calls upon Jesus Christ as Lord.

- **Worship, in Spirit and in Truth** - Though the Lutheran State Church in Iceland offers the comfort of traditionalism, it is largely void of the life-giving freedom found from embracing God's Word. Pray that this false religious security would not keep the people God is calling to himself from hearing and receiving the truth of God's Word.

- **For God to equip the church** - In a culture that prides itself on being the most progressive country in Europe, Icelanders can focus on what the Bible has to say about social issues, such as abortion and homosexuality. Pray that God would equip the church to exhibit the grace of Christ while simultaneously proclaiming what is true from God's Word.

3. For the Love of God to Increase

- **Community within the church** - Icelanders are known for being a warm, friendly, but isolated people. Pray that in the church, friendships and familial relationships would flourish and abound so that others see the love of Christ and are drawn to him. "Beloved, if God so loved us, we also ought to love one another." (1 John 4:11)

- **Unity** - Pray with the words of Philippians 1, that the church in Iceland would be faithful to preach the Word, "standing firm in one spirit, with one mind striving side by side for the faith of the gospel." (Phil. 1:27)

- **New family members welcomed into the household of God** - Pray that God would save many and bring them to himself through the spread of the good news of Christ come to save sinners! Pray that God would open the eyes of many and would draw them to the fellowship of the local church, so they might grow in Christlikeness and maturity.

- **Through the maturing of his children** - "Faith comes by hearing, and hearing by the Word of God" (Rom 10:17). Pray that the seeds of God's Word would sink deep into the hearts of His children, and that as a result, they would grow into maturity and the "measure of the stature of the fullness of Christ" (Eph 4:13).

After this I looked, and behold, a great multitude that no one could number, from every nation, from all tribes and peoples and languages, standing before the throne and before the Lamb, clothed in white robes, with palm branches in their hands, and crying out with a loud voice, "Salvation belongs to our God who sits on the throne, and to the Lamb!"
-Revelation 7:9-10

APPENDIX A

A BRIEF SUMMARY OF NORSE MYTHOLOGY

I have pieced together this brief retelling of a few Norse myths from the anthology *Norse Mythology: Tales of the Gods, Sagas, and Heroes* and Neil Gaiman's *Norse Mythology*. I am not the seasoned writer that Neil Gaiman is, and so I would encourage you to check out his work for a more complete retelling of Norse myth (not to mention his audiobook recording is fantastic!).

The Creation of the World and Humankind

Before the world began, there was a vast expanse and an abyss called Ginnungagap. On one side of the gap, the frost of Niflheim split into twelve years, some of which flowed as waterfalls into the abyss. On the other side of the gap, the flames of Muspelheim sparked and spurted into the abyss. The ice of Niflheim and the fire of Muspelheim were imbued with a kind of power so that when the two collided, magic happened.

Like an electric shock, Muspelheim's flames sent sparks that ignited the mist and formed the first giant, Ymir. Then the mist and fire collided again and formed a cow named Audhumla, and the giant fed on her milk. The frozen mist of Niflheim was so filled with power that as Audhumla licked the air, the first god came to be. Borr (or Bur) was fair and strong, and became the father of Odin, Vili and Ve. You see, the very first giant Ymir brought forth two giant-children, one boy, named Mimir, and one girl, named Bestla. Bestla married Borr and gave birth to their sons.[1]

Odin and his two brothers then banded together to slay the giant Ymir, and his dead body became the foundation of the earth. As the *Poetic Edda* says: "from Ymir's flesh / the earth was formed / and from his bones the hills, / the heaven from the skull / of that ice-cold giant, / and from his blood the sea."[2] Even his thoughts became melancholy clouds, and his skill trapped sparks of Muspelheim that men call stars.[3]

Once the earth was formed, the gods moved to the realm of Asgard, which resides above the earth and heaven. One day, Odin and his brothers Vili and Ve, were walking by the sea when they encountered one ash tree and one elm tree. From these trees they created the first human beings, man and woman, and named them Ask and Embla. The first human beings were not strong like the gods, but "nearly powerless" and "void of destiny."[4] They had no spirit, sense, blood, motive, or power until the gods crafted it into them, "Spirit gave Odin, / sense gave Hoenis, / blood gave Lodur / and goodly color."[5]

The world of Norse myth is divided into nine realms. The gods inhabit the highest realm, Asgard, while humans occupy the middle realm of Midgard. The frozen realm of the giants is Jötunheim, and Hel is the realm of fiery destruction reserved for Hella, the goddess of death. The rest of the realms appear less frequently in the sagas and are not worth naming here. Finally, the bifrost bridge and the world tree connect the nine realms together—the bifrost encompasses them like a rainbow, and the world tree intersects through the center of each realm. Life springs up through the world tree, which sustains all the creatures in all the realms, and is quite literally a *tree of life*.

Odin seeks wisdom to save the world

When trouble threatened the worlds of Asgard and Midgard, Odin returned to the land of Mimir to ask the giant for one look into his pool of wisdom. Odin tried everything he could think of to bribe the giant into allowing him to gaze into the pool—he offered all the gold in his kingdom, swords, and shields. The giant declined and told Odin that "wisdom can only be gained by suffering and sacrifice."[6] Willing to gain wisdom at all costs, Odin sacrificed one of his eyes and submitted himself to whatever suffering Mimir required.

And so, Odin hung on the world tree for nine days so that he could receive the *word of truth*.

He hung on a tree at the center of the world, and as the myth goes—he offered himself to himself as a sacrifice. He was wounded with a spear and was not offered any food or any drink while he hung. As he neared death, Odin applied himself to learn the runes of wisdom. With each gasp of pain and agony hanging on the world tree, he neared closer to the source of wisdom and saw the stories and songs of old. On the point of death, he received wisdom in the form of runes, words, facts, and "began to bear fruit, / and to know many things, / to grow and well thrive: / word by word / I sought out words, / fact by fact / I sought out facts."[7]

Ragnarok, the end of the world

At a gathering of all the gods in Asgard, the god of trickery, Loki, tricked Baldr's blind brother Höðr to throw an arrow at Baldr, which struck his heart and killed him. His death sparks the events that lead to Ragnarok, where Thor, Odin, and the good gods face off against Loki, Hella, and an army of frost giants.

Here, some retellings of Ragnarok place this end of the world battle in the past, where others place it in the future. I personally find the version set in the future more compelling, so that is how I've written it here.

Loki and his army of frost giants will storm the gates of Asgard to fight all the gods of Wisdom, Strength, and Justice. In this apocalyptic battle between the gods of good and evil, both sides neutralize the other as the strongest of gods—even Odin and Thor—simultaneously slay their enemies and die in the fight. As the dust settles from Ragnarok, all the gods and men (except for one man and one woman) will be destroyed and the earth will rest in peace.

But one god will return—Baldr. He will rise from the dead and reign as the god of beauty, purity, goodness, and truth. Once Ragnarok ends, Baldr will return to restore the earth and humankind under his rule.

Analysis of the stories
Though these stories are not looked upon as religious stories, they weave together a cultural fabric that informs the way Icelanders view the world. These stories make up a piece of how Icelanders understand creation, redemption, and the end of the world, even subconsciously.

APPENDIX B

ICELANDERS IN FILM
AND MUSIC

As a people, Icelanders are incredibly creative individuals, especially considering the size of their population. In the past two decades, Icelandic artists have been recognized for their talents on the world stage, and their work provides a snapshot of Icelandic culture.

Icelanders are making their way into the realm of film with great success. Take for example the Swedish-produced Millenium series, *The Girl with the Dragon Tattoo (2009)*, *The Girl who Played with Fire (2009)*, and *The Girl who Kicked the Hornets Nest (2009)*. Noomi Rapace, the actress who plays Lisbeth Salander in all three films is Swedish, but grew up in Iceland and speaks fluent Icelandic. Her performance was widely praised and she won the Best Actress prize at Sweden's prestigious Guldbagge Awards. The new American installment of the next book in the series, *The Girl in the Spider's Web (2019)*, features Icelandic actor Sverrir Guðnason as lead role Mikael Blomkvist, who will replace Daniel Craig from the 2011 version.

Icelanders have also proven their talent in film and television score composition, and for more than just films produced in-country. For example, the large-scale production of crime drama *Broadchurch* (2013-2017) showcases David Tennant and Olivia Colman in a tiny village on the Scottish coast. This modern murder mystery unravels beautifully with the melodic and melancholy notes of Ólafur Arnalds' compositions. An Icelandic composer, Arnalds' music highlights the northernness so fitting in the show. His ending theme also includes Icelandic band, Arnór Dan, for a moving conclusion.

In 2010, American animated film *How to Train your Dragon* highlighted the music of Icelandic singer and songwriter Jónsi, the stage name for Jón Þór "Jónsi" Birgisson. Jónsi's otherworldly music features prominently in the entire *How to Train your Dragon* trilogy, with the final installment released in 2019. *Jónsi* also composed and performed the soundtrack for the film *We bought a Zoo* in 2011, which featured leads Scarlett Johansson and Matt Damon in a story about a single dad on a mission to restore joy to his young daughter by buying and restoring a dilapidated zoo. Jónsi's lighthearted music score follows the endearing story with songs such as "Boy Lilikoi" and "Hoppípolla" (which translates to 'jumping in puddles'). Both of these songs were previously recorded and released on two separate albums. Jónsi follows the trend of other Icelandic musicians, who are part of multiple bands. Jónsi is the lead singer for post-rock Icelandic band Sigur Rós, named after his sister Sigurrós Elín, and has collaborated on a number of albums released under the name Jónsi & Alex.

Other famous Icelandic bands include the Reykjavík-based popular alternative group, *Of Monsters and Men*, which topped the charts in America, Ireland, Iceland, and parts of Europe with their song "Little Talks" on album *Dirty Paws*, released in 2011. Even today, the song has more than 350 million listens on Spotify. The band's musicians are all Icelandic, and include lead singer and guitarist Nanna Bryndís Hilmarsdóttir, singer and guitarist Ragnar "Raggi" Þórhallsson, guitarist Brynjar Leifsson, drummer Arnar Rósenkranz Hilmarsson and bassist Kristján Páll Kristjánsson. Their most recent album *Fever Dream* was released in 2019.

And while Reykjavík musicians such as *Of Monsters and Men* are gaining traction internationally for their music, the city itself is worth mentioning for its creative atmosphere. In downtown Reykjavík the sidewalks themselves inspire creativity. On one corner, a multi-colored pastel sea dragon winds its way along the sidewalk and sports a fluffy tail and fanciful head. Houses are painted in bright colors, from bright yellow to deep turquoise and fire-engine red. Many houses are decked out with street art, not in the style of graffiti, but feature creatures you might expect to find in a children's book written by Dr. Seuss. Mermaids, sea dragons, birds, and mythical animals that combine features from a few different animals peek out around street corners and show their faces along parking spaces.

Icelanders are incredibly creative as a people, and there are far too many creative geniuses to highlight here. For a cursory overview of a few of my personal favorites, you will find specific examples of movies, music, and literature in the additional resources page at the back of this book.

APPENDIX C

ICELANDIC ALPHABET & PRONUNCIATION GUIDE

Icelanders are proud of their literary heritage as well they should be! Icelandic is the purest Germainic language currently spoken in the world, and is a direct descendent of Old Norse. Below are pronunciation examples for each letter of the Icelandic alphabet. You will notice two new letters—Ðð ("Eth") and Þþ ("Thorn")—which are entirely unique to the Icelandic language. Fun fact, they used to be present in ancient versions of Old English.

Aa	a	-	Pronounced "ah" as in father.
Áá	á	-	Pronounced "ow" as in cow.
Bb	bé	-	Pronounced "buh" as in boat to be gin a word. Otherwise "puh" as in speak.
Dd	dé	-	Pronounced "duh" as in door to be gin a word. Otherwise "tuh" as in stuck.
Ðð	eð	-	Pronounced as a hard "th" as in father or the.
Ee	e	-	Pronounced "eh" as in effect.
Éé	é	-	Pronounced "yeh" as in yeti, yes, or yellow.
Ff	eff	-	Pronounced "feh" as in felt to begin and end words. Otherwise, F is tricky – sounds like "vuh" between vowels, as in hover. Before L or N, pronounced "puh" as in split.

Gg	ge	-	Pronounced "guh" as in golf to begin a word. Otherwise, G is tricky – be tween consonants pronounced "kuh" as in sparkle, before a T as "khuh" in Bach, and between vow els as a soft "ghuh" as in give, but without allowing your tongue to touch the roof of your mouth.
Hh	há	-	Pronounced "huh" as in hello. Be fore a V, sounds like "kuh" as in mikvah.
Ii	i	-	Pronounced "ih" as in sister. See "Y" below.
Íí	í	-	Pronounced "ee" as in see. Can be swapped for Ý in some words, see below.
Jj	joð	-	Pronounced as a "yoh" as in yogurt or yolk.
Kk	ká	-	Pronounced "kuh" as in kite. Before a T, pronounced "khuh" as in Bach.
Ll	ell	-	Pronounced "leh" as in love.
Mm	emm	-	Pronounced "mm" as in melt.
Nn	enn	-	Pronounced "nn" as in nap or nut.
Oo	o	-	Pronounced as a short "oh" as in old or boy.
Óó	ó	-	Pronounced as a long "ō" as in snow.
Pp	pé	-	Pronounced as a breathy "puh" as in puff.
Rr	err	-	Pronounced "hurr" with a soft rolled R, think about the way that a cat purrs, and the sounds or the "t" and "r" combination in water or the "d" and "r" combination in ladder.
Ss	ess	-	Pronounced "ss" but with an added whistle, as in hiss, grass, or sell.

Tt	té	-	Pronounced "tuh" as in tale or typo (the bane of a writer's existence!).
Uu	u	-	Pronounced "üh" as in book or put.
Úú	ú	-	Pronounced "oo" as in croon or soothe.
Vv	vaff	-	Pronounced "vuh" as in vest or silver.
Xx	ex	-	Pronounced "x" as in tax or relax.
Yy	ufsilon y		Pronounced identically to "I" above, "ih" as in hymn or rhythm.
Ýý	ufsilon ý		Pronounced identically to "Í" above, "ee" as in spree or key.
Þþ	þorn	-	Pronounced "thuh" as in theater (theatre for the Brits!) or earth.
Æ æ	æ	-	Pronounced "īy" as in hi, bye, or bonsai.
Öö	ö	-	Pronounced like the "uh" in urban or the "ih" in girl, but with a silent "r" like in a British accent.

SOURCES

Use of the Bible, the Holy Scriptures

Unless otherwise stated, all Scripture quotations are from the ESV® Bible (The Holy Bible, English Standard Version®), copyright © 2001 by Crossway, a publishing ministry of Good News Publishers. Used by permission. All rights reserved.

Chapter 1 - The Land of Fire & Ice

1. Statistics Iceland, "Populations by religious and life stance organizations 1998-2019." (Web Publication, May 18, 2019). Accessed June 27, 2019.
https://px.hagstofa.is/pxen/pxweb/en/Samfelag/Samfelag_menning_5_trufelog/MAN10001.px

Chapter 2 - A Brief History of Iceland

1. Craigie, William A. The Icelandic Sagas. Cambridge, UK New York: Cambridge Univ Press, 2011, page 23.

2. Karlsson, Gunnar. The History of Iceland. Minneapolis, Minn: University of Minnesota Press, 2000, page 14.

3. Fell, Michael. And Some Fell into Good Soil: A History of Christianity in Iceland. New York: Peter Lang, 1999, page 22.

4. Fell, page 23.

5. Ashliman, D. L. "Iceland Accepts Christianity: Abstracted from Njal's Saga." University of Pittsburgh, Pittsburgh, PA, February 19, 2001. Accessed Mar. 9,

2020. https://www.pitt.edu/~dash/njal100.html

*If Norse mythology intrigues you, I have summarized some pertinent myths in Appendix A.

6. Karlsson, Gunnar. The History of Iceland. Minneapolis, Minn: University of Minnesota Press, 2000, page 96.

7. Fell, pages 73-74.

8. Karlsson, page 92.

9. Karlsson, page 102.

10. Karlsson, page 115.

11. Karlsson, page 116.

12. Karlsson, page 128.

13. Karlsson, page 128.

14. Karlsson, page 129.

15. Karlsson, page 136.

16. Fell, page 91.

17. Hallgrimur Petursson. "The Purple Dress and the Crown of Thorns" in Passíuslmár or Hymns of the Passion, quoted in Gunnar Karlsson, pages 147-148.

18. Fell, page 105.

19. Fell, page 108.

20. Fell, page 154.

21. Jón Vídalín, Vídalínspostilla (1995 edition, page

493), quoted in Michael Fell, And Some Fell into Good Soil: A History of Christianity in Iceland. New York: Peter Lang, 1999, page 154.

22. Karlsson, page 129.

23. Karlsson, page 133.

24. Karlsson, page 144.

25. Karlsson, page 177.

26. Karlsson, page 180.

27. "Iceland rumored plan for the Annexation of the Island to the United States." Ashburton Guardian (Ashburton, New Zealand), Mar. 4, 1888.

28. Karlsson, page 236.

29. Pétursson, Pétur. Church and Social Change: A Study of the Secularization Process in Iceland since 1830, Third ed. Reykjavik: 2017, page 122.

30. Helgi Guðnisson and Aron Hinriksson (Co-pastors of Hvítasunnukirkjan Filidelfia, "Brotherly Love Pentecostal Church" in Reykjavík). In discussion with the author, Jul. 3, 2019.

31. Helgi Guðnisson (Co-pastor of Hvítasunnukirkjan Fi lidelfia, "Brotherly Love Pentecostal Church" in Reykjavík). In discussion with the author, Dec. 10, 2019.

*Independent Churches are not affiliated with the National Lutheran Church in Iceland.

32. Helgi Guðnisson and Aron Hinriksson (Co-pastors of Hvítasunnukirkjan Filidelfia, "Brotherly Love Pen-

tecostal Church" in Reykjavík). In discussion with the author, Jul. 3, 2019.

33. Helgi Guðnisson (Co-pastor of Hvítasunnukirkjan Flidelfia, "Brotherly Love Pentecostal Church" in Reykjavík). Emphasis provided by Helgi. In discussion with the author, Dec. 10, 2019.

34. Karlsson, page 322.

35. Gunnarsson, Valur. "From the US Army to Army of Me." The Reykjavík Grapevine (Reykjavík, Iceland), Jun. 14, 2012. Accessed Mar. 9, 2020. www.grapevine.is/icelan dic-culture/literature-and-poetry/2012/06/14/ from-the-us-army-to-army-of-me/

Chapter 3 - Current Cultural Factors

1. Brown, Abbie Farewell and Sarah Powers Bradish. Norse Mythology: Tales of the Gods, Sagas and Heroes. London: Arcturus Publishing Limited, 2018, page 28.

2. Wessén, E., "Award Ceremony Speech." From Nobel Lectures, Literature 1901-1967, Editor Horst Frenz, Elsevier Publishing Company, Amsterdam, 1969. Accessed Mar. 9, 2020. https://www.nobelprize.org/prizes/literature/1955/ceremony-speech/

3. Banner of Liberty (New York), Jun. 20, 1860, page 197.

4. "Iceland - Adult (15+) literacy rate." World Data Atlas. Knoema. Accessed Mar. 9, 2020. www.knoema.com/atlas/Iceland/topics/Education/Literacy/Adult-literacy-rate

5. Kolomichuk, Veronika (born in Iceland, raised in the United States). In discussion with the author, Oct. 9, 2018.

6. Kyzer, Larissa. "Icelandic Names will no longer be Gendered." Iceland Review, Jun. 22, 2019.
Accessed Mar. 3, 2020. www.icelandreview.com/news/icelandic-names-will-no-longer-be-gendered/?fbclid=IwAR3Z9-zYG_632I0BN0-bE5LjSyEeJ_iHo70p-4PaY5VmUuDaCUfz2CG3vWJQ

7. Chamie, Joseph. "Out of Wedlock Births Rise Worldwide." YaleGlobal Online, Mar. 16, 2017. Accessed Mar. 9, 2020. https://yaleglobal.yale.edu/content/out-wedlock-births- rise-worldwide

8. "Countries where Corporal Punishment in the home is Outlawed." World Atlas. Accessed Mar. 9, 2020. www.worldatlas.com/articles/countries-where-corporal-punishment-in-the-home-is-outlawed.html

9. Gunnarsson, Gunnar Ingi (Icelandic pastor and church planter). In discussion with the author, Oct. 13, 2018.

10. Pierce, Benjamin Mills. "A Report on the resources of Iceland and Greenland." U.S. State Department, Washington: Government Printing Office, 1868, page 17. Accessed Mar. 9, 2020. https://books.google.com/books?id=U9lIAAAAMAAJ&pg=PP13#v=onepage&q&f=false

11. Helliwell, J., R. Layard and J. Sachs. "World Happiness Report 2019." Sustainable Development Solutions Network. New York, Mar. 20, 2019. Accessed Mar. 9, 2020. https://worldhappiness.report/ed/2019/

12. McCarthy, Niall. "The World's Biggest Consumers of Anti-Depressants." Forbes, Nov. 16, 2015. Accessed July 31, 2019. https://www.forbes.com/sites/niallmccarthy/2015/11/16/the-worlds-biggest-consumers-of-antidepressants/#32511f9a6c06

13. Gould, Skye and Lauren F. Friedman. "The top countries for antidepressant use is rising sharply around the world." Business Insider, Oct. 6, 2016. Accessed Mar. 9, 2020. https://www.businessinsider.com/countries-larg   est-antidepressant-drug-users-2016-11

14. "Teenage Suicides (15-19)." Organization for Economic and Cooperative Development, Oct. 17, 2017. Accessed Mar. 9, 2020. https://www.oecd.org/els/fami ly/CO_4_4_Teenage-Suicide.pdf

15. Bowers, Jeffrey. "Staff Pick Premiere: 'Whale Valley'." (Interview with Guðmundur Arnar Guðmundsson) Vimeo, Dec. 14, 2016. Accessed Mar. 9, 2020. https://vimeo.com/blog/post/staff-pick-premiere-whale-valley

16. Gunnarsson, Gunnar Ingi (Icelandic pastor and church planter). In discussion with the author, Oct. 13, 2018.

Chapter 4 - Barriers to Gospel Progress

1. Karlsdóttir, Kristín Björg (Icelander and member of Loft sofan Baptistakirkja). In discussion with the author, Aug.17, 2018.

2. Statistics Iceland, "Populations by religious and life stance organizations 1998-2019." (Web Publication, May 18,2019). Accessed June 27, 2019. https://px.hagstofa.is/pxen/pxweb/en/Samfelag/Samfelag__menning__5_trufelog/MAN10001.px

3. Pétursson, Pétur. Church and Social Change: A Study of the Secularization Process in Iceland since 1830. Reykjavik: Pétur Pétursson, 2017, page 63.

4. Thorsteinsson, Thorsteinn, Iceland 1930: A Handbook Published on the Fortieth Anniversary of Lands-

banki Íslands (National Bank of Iceland). 2nd ed. Reyk-javík: Ríkisprentsmiðjan Gutenberg, 1930, page 120.

5. Gunnarsson, Gunnar Ingi (Icelandic pastor and church planter). In discussion with the author, Oct. 13, 2018.

6. Pétursson, page 120.
7. Pétursson, page 37.

8. Iceland Magazine Staff Writers. "How much is the average wage in Iceland?" Iceland Magazine. August 29, 2018. Accessed March 24, 2020. https://icelandmag.is/article/how-much-average-wage-iceland

9. Fontaine, Andie. "The Exodus from the Church." The Reyk javik Grapevine. September 7, 2018. Accessed June 28,2019. https://grapevine.is/mag/articles/2018/09/07/the-exodus-from-the-church/

10. "Civilian Confirmation." The Ethical Humanist Association. May 8, 2018. Accessed March 24, 2020. http://sidmennt.is/2018/08/05/civil-confirmation-in-iceland/

11. Jónsdóttir, Guðrún Hrönn (Icelander and member of Loftstofan Baptistakirkja). In discussion with the author, Jun. 26, 2019.

12. Hólm, Sólveig (Icelandic ceramics artist). In discussion with the author, Jul. 1, 2019.

13. Helgason, Magnús Sveinn. "Heathens against hate: Exclusive interview with the high priest of the Icelandic Pagan Association." Iceland Magazine. July 25, 2015. Accessed March 24, 2020. https://icelandmag.is/article/heathens-against-hate-exclusive-interview-high-priest-icelandic-pagan-association

Chapter 5 - The Future of the Church in Iceland

1. Since the service I attended was entirely in English, the liturgy was taken from the Anglican Book of Common Prayer.

2. Bjarnason, Bjarni Þór (Icelander and vicar for the national Lutheran church). In discussion with the author, Jun. 30, 2019.

3. Statistics Iceland, "Populations by religious and life stance organizations 1998-2019." (Web Publication, May 18, 2019). Accessed June 27, 2019. https://px.hagstofa.is/pxen/pxweb/en/Samfelag/Samfelag__menning__5_trufelog/MAN10001.px

4. Jónsson, Kjartan (Icelander and priest for the national Lutheran church). In discussion with the author, Jul. 3, 2019.

5. Gunnarsson, Gunnar Ingi (Icelandic pastor and church planter). In discussion with the author, Oct. 13, 2018.

6. Jónsdóttir, Guðrún Hrönn (Icelander and member of Loftstofan Baptistakirkja). In discussion with the author, Jun. 26, 2019.

Chapter 6 - The Future of the Church in Iceland

1. Name protected for safety.

2. Kolomichuk, Veronika (American church member with family in Iceland). In discussion with the author, Oct. 9, 2018.

3. Trading Economics, "Iceland Personal Income Tax Rate: 1995 to 2020 Data." (Web Publication). Accessed April 27, 2019.   https://tradingeconomics.com/ice-

land/personal-income-tax-rate

4. To contact Logan Douglas and other members of The Iceland Project team, please see the contact information provided in the Additional Resources section.

Appendix A - Norse Mythology

1. Brown, Abbie Farewell, Sarah Powers Bradish, and Mary Litchfield. Norse Mythology: Tales of the Gods, Sagas, and Heroes. Arcturus Publishing: London, 2018, pages 33-34.

2. Brown, page 35.

3. Brown, page 35

4. Brown, page 36

5. Brown, page 36

6. Brown, page 19.

7. Brown, page 19. Quotation from "Odin's Rune Song" in Benjamin Thorpe's 1866 translation of Saemund's Poetic Edda.

ADDITIONAL RESOURCES

There are so many fantastic resources out there to give you a full picture of Iceland's rich cultural heritage, and still more reveal what it's like to partner with gospel-centered ministry in Iceland! Below, I've included just the highlight reel in this quick-reference guide.

Churches & Church Planting Networks
- The Iceland Project - www.theicelandproject.org
- Loftstofan Baptistakirkja (Upper Room Baptist Church) - www.loftstofan.is
- Redeemer City Church - www.redeemercityreykjavik.com
- Hvítasunnukirkjan Fíladelfía (Pentecostal Church of Brotherly Love) - www.filadelfia.is
- New City Network - Church planting network with connections to church plants in Iceland - www.newcityplanting.org
- Radstock Network - International Church Planting Network - www.radstock.org/churches

Videos from Christians in Iceland
- Christian by Default - a documentary of the state of the church in Iceland (2016) - https://www.youtube.com/watch?v=YOZ39oVDuhw
- Loftstofan Baptistakirkja promo video - https://www.youtube.com/watch?v=i7qI69POZhE&ct=t%28Y%29
- Redeemer City Church promo video - https://www.redeemercityreykjavik.com/video

Culture and Media in Iceland
Media
- The Reykjavík Grapevine - a popular news and culture magazine, written entirely in English - www.grapevine.is

- Iceland Magazine - also written in English, this magazine provides unusual stories and travel tips - www.icelandmag.is

Music

- KALEO - On all music platforms or - www.officialkaleo.com
- Music video: KALEO's "Vor í Vaglaskógi" features some beautifully pastoral scenes from Iceland and captures some of the Icelandic soul - https://www.youtube.com/watch?v=Da5qQD_RpEQ
- Music video: KALEO's "Save Yourself" performed live on an iceberg - https://www.youtube.com/watch?v=oCi0RHLrauU
- Sigur Rós - On all music platforms or - www.sigurros.com/
- Of Monsters and Men - On all music platforms or - www.ofmonstersandmen.com
- Jónsi - featured in the soundtrack of How to Train your Dragon, and available on all music platforms - www.jonsi.com
- Ólafur Arnalds - soundtrack composer of shows such as Broadchurch - www.olafurarnalds.com

Movies & TV

- For a review of a variety of critically-acclaimed Icelandic short films check out - https://www.shortoftheweek.com/channels/iceland
- Full-length Milk and Blood - https://vimeo.com/82631920
- Full-length Whale Valley - https://www.youtube.com/watch?v=rvPiCpyW17M

Literature

- Halldór Laxness - Nobel Prize winning author for Salka Valka (1931). Other titles include Independent People (1935), World Light (1940), and The Happy Warriors (1952).

Norse Mythology

- For an updated English re-telling of Norse Mythology, see Neil Gaiman's Norse Mythology.
- For a historical comparison of the sagas by a Cambridge scholar, try William A. Craigie's The Icelandic Sagas.
- For a quick summary of all Norse myths, try the volume Norse Mythology: Tales of the Gods, Sagas and Heroes, edited by Abbie Farewell Brown, Sarah Powers Bradish, and others.

Education in Iceland

- The University of Iceland - www.english.hi.is/university_of_iceland
- Free Icelandic Language classes - the University of Iceland - www.icelandiconline.com

Want to get in touch?

- Connect with the Iceland Project Team! www.theicelandproject.org/contact

Made in the USA
Middletown, DE
25 November 2020